GOD'S NOT DONE
WITH YOUR CHURCH

Available in the Replant Series

GOD'S NOT DONE
WITH YOUR CHURCH

MARK HALLOCK

 ACOMA PRESS

God's Not Done with Your Church: Finding Hope and New Life through Replanting

Copyright © 2017 by Mark Hallock

Published 2017 by Acoma Press

a publishing ministry of the Calvary Family of Churches

> 40 W. Littleton Blvd. Suite 210, PMB 215
> Littleton, CO 80120
>
> www.acomapress.org

Unless otherwise noted, all Bible references are from the ESV® Bible (The Holy Bible, English Standard Version®), copyright © 2001 by Crossway, a publishing ministry of Good News Publishers. Used by permission. All rights reserved.

Requests for information should be addressed to:

> The Calvary Family of Churches
> 40 W. Littleton Blvd. Suite 210, PMB 215
> Littleton, CO 80120
>
> www.thecalvary.org
> office@thecalvary.org

Cover Design & Interior Layout: Evan Skelton

First Printing, 2017

Printed in the United States of America

Paperback ISBN: 978-0-9988597-4-3
PDF ISBN: 978-0-9988597-5-0

To those who have remained faithful to the Lord and their local church, even in the darkest and most discouraging of times. Thank you for leaning on his grace and hanging on. The Lord is honored in you.

CONTENTS

ACKNOWLEDGMENTS

I want to thank a few important individuals who played a vital role in the shaping and writing of this book.

I want to thank my wonderful wife, Jenna, and my children Zoe and Eli. Thank you for your constant encouragement in my life and ministry.

Thank you to Ruth Piotrowski who sacrificed many hours to make this book what it is. I am so grateful. The joy of the Lord is all over you, my friend.

Thank you to Evan Skelton, a great designer and editor, but an even better friend.

Thank you to my mom and dad for teaching me to love the local church. More than that, for modeling what it looks like to love the local church with a steady commitment, through both highs and lows, mountain tops and valleys.

Special thanks to the following friends who added so much to this project: Dave and Nancy Elliott, Bart and Kim Waress, Jeff and Tyann Declue, Kenny and Sue Bridges, Richard and Krysti Derby, Nathan Rose, Butch Schierman, Jon Kempf, Mark Clifton, the NAMB replant team, and my Calvary Family of Churches' brothers and sisters.

I praise God for the gift it is to serve alongside each of you.

Soli Deo Gloria.

FORWARD

Churches across North America are dying at an alarming rate. Approximately 100,000 churches are in a downward spiral that will likely result in death unless something drastic changes. In my own denomination, the Southern Baptist Convention, approximately 70-75% of churches are plateaued or declining and another 10-15% are at risk of shutting their doors permanently. For Christians, these are not merely statistics; these are congregations that are failing to display the transforming power of the gospel, as well as reach their communities with the good news of Jesus.

If you find yourself in a situation where your church is close to calling it quits, be assured that there is hope. The book you hold in your hands is a practical resource that can prevent your church from becoming one of the statistics mentioned above. In *God's Not Done with Your Church* pastor and church replanter, Mark Hallock, provides struggling churches with the vision, strategy, and knowledge needed to help them thrive again and reach others in Jesus' name.

I can think of no one more suitable for and qualified to write a book such as this. The first time I met Mark, he shared with me the miraculous story of how the Lord turned around his church, Calvary Baptist Church. After over half a century of ministry, Calvary was months away from shutting its doors permanently. But Mark believed that God was not finished with his church. He knew that the Lord is a God who delights to bring beauty from ashes and life from death—all for the glory of his name. Of course, the changes Mark implemented were not easy or simplistic, but now (by God's grace) Calvary is a thriving congregation reaching unbelievers, transforming their community, and helping revitalize other churches.

I don't know what the future of your church looks like, but I do know that God doesn't want your church to die; there is nothing about a dying church that brings him honor. So let me encourage you to prayerfully read this book with an open heart and a teachable spirit, trusting that God is not done with your church.

Nathan Rose
Senior Pastor, Liberty Baptist Church
Liberty, Missouri

Chapter 1

WHAT IS CHURCH REPLANTING?

It seems like just yesterday that the Lord called my family and I to leave a very comfortable, life-giving ministry that we loved in order to lead and shepherd Calvary Baptist Church in Englewood, Colorado. At the time, Calvary was a church of 30 sweet folks who loved Jesus but were weary and ready to close the doors of the church for good. They needed serious help. They needed help that had to come from the Lord himself.

You see, Calvary had once been a healthy, vibrant congregation that multiplied and sent members out to plant other churches. Several churches in the Denver metro area exist today because at one time Calvary had the vision, passion, and faith to plant new congregations. However, like so many other churches over the years, Calvary slowly began to decline. The community around the church began to change. Families began to move away. Older members were passing away. A few pastors came in who were more focused on their own agenda than on God's. And sadly, over time, Calvary began to die. But the Lord wasn't done with this church. He had not given up on this church!

Friend, I'm assuming you're reading this book because your church is in decline like Calvary once was. I'm sure that you've invested a great deal of your life into your church. You've poured your heart, energy, time, resources, sweat, and tears into doing the Lord's work. And it's painful and devastating to see the church slipping away rather than growing and teeming with life. Is this the end? It doesn't have to be! There is help for churches like yours. Know that I am cheering for your church, and my prayer is that you would not lose hope or give up!

The truth is, God has not given up on most churches that many of us would have given up on a long time ago. The Lord loves struggling churches and receives much glory when bringing them back to life and vibrancy. This includes your church! And the amazing thing is that he invites us to be a part of it.

REVITALIZATION VS. REPLANTING: WHAT'S THE DIFFERENCE?

If your church is currently struggling, know that you are not alone. Unfortunately, statistics show that the church is in decline nationwide. For example, according to the Hartford Institute of Religion Research, only 20 percent of Americans attend church weekly. Twenty percent! Also, within the Southern Baptist Convention alone, an average of 17 Southern Baptist churches close their doors for good *every Sunday*, leaving underserved and unreached neighborhoods in cities across North America. With these statistics alone in mind (and there are many more), you can quickly see that not only are we in need of new, healthy churches in North America, but we are also in desperate need of revitalizing and replanting declining and dying churches. So, what exactly are we meaning when we talk about church revitalization and church replanting?

With the concerns of your own church on the forefront of your mind, the terms church revitalization and church replanting may become a larger part of your vocabulary. You may already have a basic understanding of the terms, or they may be completely new to you. So what's the difference between the two? Let's start by considering church revitalization as many of us could take an educated guess on what it means simply based on the name. But hopefully we know it's more than just changing the carpet in a sanctuary or adding some new worship songs! The reality is revitalization is needed in almost every church in our country today.

In church revitalization, the hope and intent is to help a plateaued or declining church get healthy again so that it can become a unified, vibrant, disciple-making congregation on mission to reach their surrounding community with the gospel. Revitalization is a work only God can do through the power of the Holy Spirit as he works in the heart of a church and its members.

Typically in a revitalization context, a church knows they need help, but they may be unaware of just how *much* help they need. This type of church still has *a lot* of fight left in them. They have a functional building and enough money and people who are able to hold out for several more years without hitting the panic button. While money, people, and a building can all be great blessings to a church in need of revitalization, these can also help to create a false sense of security which prevents a church from making the necessary changes to become healthy and growing again. In contrast to replanting, the congregation we are describing has no intention of becoming a new or different church; however, it does desire to hire a pastor who will help lead them back to health and vitality.

There are typically differing mentalities among the congregants within a declining church like this. There are probably some who are saying, "We've really got to do something now! We've got to make some major changes or we're going to die." There may be others who are saying, "Meh, things aren't great, but we're doing okay." And, most likely, there is a third group of folks who are saying, "We're just fine. We don't need to change anything. Are you kidding me? Things are great!" So these are the three typical mindsets among the church members of this struggling church. As you can imagine, a church revitalization brings with it not only great challenges, but also potential opportunities for great Kingdom work.

WHAT IS CHURCH REPLANTING?

Now that you've gotten a glimpse into church revitalization, let's put the focus mainly on church replanting. Contrary to what you may have heard, church replanting is **not** the same thing as church revitalization. There are important distinctions. Think of it this way: Church replanting is a specific strategy or approach *to* church revitalization. Broadly speaking, if church revitalization is concerned with helping plateaued or declining churches experience new life and vitality, church replanting is one of the most biblical, God-honoring, and effective strategies for actually making it happen. For the purposes of this book, we will define church replanting as the process by which an existing church is re-launched as a new church, with new leadership (a new replanting pastor), new name, new identity, new governance, new ministry approach and overall new philosophy of ministry.

Pastor and church replanting strategist, Jeff DeClue, gives a helpful analogy of what replanting is like:

> Imagine that you were given a beautiful plant. Everyone that came to your house complimented you on its size, health, vibrancy, the breathtaking fragrance. Now one day you noticed the plant was changing. Its leaves were turning pale yellow and the plant looked slightly withered. You didn't forget to water it. Maybe someone else watered it too much. Maybe it isn't getting enough light. You love this plant and you will do whatever it takes to save it. If you don't act now it is going to die. Quickly you get the plant into a new pot so that you can get back to the basics. You get food with some quality nutrients. You now can make sure it is getting ample sunshine and water. Deep green color starts to return to the leaves and its strength starts to return. It takes time but it is coming back to life. Now, replace the flower in a pot with a church in a community. This is a picture of church "replanting."

Church replanting is a very unique ministry. In church replanting, the focus is on congregations that are not simply declining, but dying—*and they know it.* These are congregations that have reached a point in which they realize they are not only sick and unhealthy, but they are nearing their death. Churches are first identified as needing to be replanted when they humbly and honestly acknowledge that they are at risk of closing their doors once and for all within two to five years if major changes are not made.

These congregations do not simply have a metaphorical cold that needs a little help to get healthy again, but rather they have some form of cancer with major surgery and treatment needed to survive. As a result, these congregations have come to a point of humble surrender. They are no longer concerned with fighting battles over such things as the color of the carpet, whether they should sing hymns or praise songs, or whether the pastor preaches in a suit or jeans. They have come to a point of humble surrender, saying, *"Lord, whatever you want to do with our church, we are all in. This is Your Church, not ours. We want to do whatever it takes to not simply survive, but thrive for the sake of the gospel, for the sake of this community."*

As Christians, we need to lock arms and fight to stop the trend of dying churches in our communities. If this is your church, be encouraged that the task of church replanting is to come alongside declining congregations like yours and lovingly and joyfully shepherd them back to health, mission, and multiplication. Al Mohler, President of The Southern Baptist Theological Seminary in Louisville, Kentucky, writes:

> One of our central tasks in the present generation is to be bold in our vision of replanting churches — helping existing churches to find new vision, new strategic focus, new passion for the gospel, new hunger for the preaching of the Word, new love for their communities, and new excitement about seeing people come to faith in Jesus. Replanting churches requires both courage and leadership skills. A passion for replanting a church must be matched by skills in ministry and a heart for helping a church to regain a vision.[1]

Indeed, the need for church replanting is great, as is the opportunity and potential. Sadly, many churches will close their doors for the final time this next Sunday. As I mentioned earlier, in the Southern Baptist Convention alone, 17 churches will close their doors for the final time *this next Sunday.* And the next week, another 17 will close. And another 17 the next week. This should break our hearts!

If you have the same concern for your own church, you surely feel even more empathy for these churches who have reached the end of their rope. Many of them are probably like yours, made up of sweet saints who love Jesus, love the Bible and love people, but have perhaps lost vision and hope for what God can do in and through them. They are sheep that need a pastor-shepherd who can know them, feed them, and lead them with passion, joy, and hope into the future. **So where do we go from here?**

A REPLANTING PATHWAY

Once a church comes to the place of humble surrender and desires to be replanted for the sake of the gospel and the glory of God, what's next? Practically, what are the next steps to begin the replanting process? Let me offer a brief overview of the primary replanting pathway we will be considering throughout this book. This pathway is one that is biblical, pastoral, missional, respectful of history, loving of people, gospel-driven, and, I firmly believe, God-honoring. It can certainly give your church a clear trajectory for starting over.

I will refer to this type of church or congregation as "dying" or "declining." Please don't let these terms discourage or offend you. God is in the business of bringing life after death! This doesn't have to mean the end for your church. There is help to be had. And here's the replanting pathway I would like to propose in a nutshell. Notice there are three primary components to this pathway. When a dying congregation joyfully chooses to be replanted, they agree to:

1. Surrender all day-to-day decision making to an outside transition team, ideally from a sending church.
2. Engage strategic outside ministry partners.
3. Call a trained replanting pastor.

What does this pathway look like practically? First, as noted above, the church needing to be replanted has already said, "We surrender. We recognize this is the Lord's church and to move forward in a healthy way, there needs to be fresh leadership. We joyfully submit to an outside transition team that can guide us into the future." This transition team could be a group of pastors, elders, deacons or other lay leaders from a particular sending church. It could be a group made up of pastors and leaders from different churches in the community. It could be a group of denominational leaders. It might be a combination of all of the above. Whoever these individuals are, the dying church has agreed to give up day-to-day decision making and oversight to this outside group of trusted leaders. They have gladly surrendered to this group to help guide them and lead them into the future.

Secondly, the congregation, along with their outside transition team, begins to engage ministry partners and churches, inviting them to be part of this new, exciting replanting vision. **The reality is that no declining church can get healthy on its own.** Declining churches need healthy churches to come alongside them, to encourage them, to help share resources with them, and to serve joyfully as partners in this new work. Radical cooperation is needed. This is the beauty of the body of Christ in action and makes much of Jesus and the gospel!

Thirdly, the congregation recognizes they need a pastor who is trained in, equipped for, and has a heart for replanting. Because replanting is a unique ministry, it takes unique leadership, including a unique type of pastor. This church needs a pastor who is a visionary shepherd. This is a pastor who is burdened to reach the lost in the community and who is willing to do whatever it takes to lead this dying church to engage the surrounding community with the love of Christ. At the same time, this congregation needs a pastor who truly loves shepherding people, both young and old, who respects and honors the history of the congregation, and who understands the unique dynamics of replanting ministry. Where does this church find such a pastor? In most cases, this replanting pastor will be identified and appointed by the outside transition team that is helping to oversee the entire replanting process for this congregation. Working with the declining congregation and potentially denominational leaders, the transition team will seek to find a replanter who they believe is a good fit for leading this congregation back to health and life.

Revitalization vs. Replanting... A Closer Look

Revitalization: A deliberate, dedicated and protracted effort to reverse the decline or death of an existing church.

- The **least** invasive approach as few major changes are made up front.

- Utilizes **existing** structures, leadership and congregants.

- May be led by an existing or **new pastor**. (Revitalization is less likely to occur successfully with a long tenured existing pastor; more likely, a new pastor will be the best way to move forward).

- Requires a **great deal of time**—the pace of change is very slow.

- **High risk** as the church may reject the leadership efforts of the pastor and leaders and ask them to leave or remove them through elevated conflict or forced termination.

- Is less likely to lead to lasting change and more likely to be a **continuation** of the same.

- Is the **least** effective approach for churches facing imminent closure.

Replant: A decision to close an existing church and re-launch as a new church, with new leadership (a new replanting pastor), new name, new identity, new governance, new ministry approach and overall new philosophy of ministry. In some cases it is not necessary to adopt a new name but simply adjust it. In some instances where a denominational label is a hindrance to reaching the community or where the name is unnecessarily long or confusing a name change may be appropriate.

- Builds on the **history/legacy** of the previous church.

- **Requires** new leadership (a new replanting pastor).

- New decision-making structure and new decision makers who handle the **daily decisions** (outside transition team).
- New **by-laws** are created and put into practice.
- Offers a break with the past (end date) and a **fresh start** for the future (launch date).
- New **identity** can create excitement, momentum, enthusiasm and interest in the community.[2]

A SENDING CHURCH?

In this book, you will be introduced to the idea of a "sending church." What is a sending church? It is a congregation that agrees to come alongside and help replant your congregation for *the long haul*. In a very real sense, the sending church serves as the sponsor or mother church for the replant. The role of this church is to pray for, encourage, and serve your congregation however they can.

The idea of a sending church is most common to hear in the context of church planting. After all, many recognize that for a church to succeed it needs more than a high-capacity pastor or compelling outreach strategy. It needs a church to foster and champion its growth. In fact, we see in the Bible that since the church first began to multiply, *churches* have been planting churches.

I think we have just as many reasons, maybe even more, to argue that churches should *replant* churches as well. Consider this analogy. You may have been in a serious accident or know someone who has been. What did the road to recovery look like after such a significant event? Who played a role in bringing you or your friend back to health? Let's list some of these people:

- **Trauma Surgeons** – practiced professionals trained to identify the most serious threats to your life and to bring you out of critical condition.

- **Nurses** – agents able to offer not only physical care but emotional, advocating on your behalf as you journey together toward recovery.

- **Physical Therapists** – coaches who push you further than you wanted or imagined you could go, in order to restore strength and mobility to muscles that had atrophied.

- **Family Members & Friends** – loved ones who bring you meals, send you cards, mow your lawn, make you laugh, and meet your needs, especially on your hardest days.

- **Counselors** – wise guides who help to process the reasons for and implications of the events in a context of safety, empathy, and correction.

Just as physical recovery takes a community of care, so does church recovery. If you want not just survival but vitality, it takes more than some paint on the walls or a new voice in the pulpit. It takes guidance, shoulder-bearing, correction, provision, encouragement, protection, and *time*. A sending church offers you this and more.

But your congregation isn't the only group in need of this kind of long-haul care. Your pastor and his family are as well. They need coaches and cheerleaders outside of your body, particularly in the first few years. Instead, many churches fail because they put it all on the pastor, who should never have to carry this kind of burden alone.

While the option of replanting through a sending church is not always possible, I am convinced it gives the potential replant its best chance for long-haul health and renewed multiplication. If you want to learn more about finding a sending church, particularly how to find the right one, take a look at the appendix I have included at the back of this book.

CAN YOU IMAGINE?

Can you imagine what would happen if we began to see large numbers of dying churches begin to pursue this kind of replanting pathway? I can tell you from experience, more and more churches are choosing to trust the Lord and take a leap of faith in this very direction. Many once-dying churches are now becoming healthy again, engaging their communities and reaching the lost with the power of Christ in new and exciting ways.

Children's Sunday School classrooms that had been empty for years are now filled with laughter and singing from little ones each and every Sunday morning. Baptism tanks that had been dry and unused for years are now being filled regularly as lost men and women experience new life in Jesus. Neighborhoods that for years had not even taken notice or cared that a church had been there are now taking notice, being impacted in countless ways through new outreach ministries making a real difference in the community. It's happening! The Lord is doing this kind of replanting work all over our country and world for his glory and the joy of his Church. **He wants to do the same in your church! God is not done with your church!**

DISCUSSION QUESTIONS

1. In what ways can your church body relate to Mark's description of Calvary Baptist Church before it was replanted?

2. What do you think has gone wrong in American churches in general? What does a healthy church look like?

3. What are some differences between church revitalization and church replanting?

4. Do you think your church needs revitalization or replanting? Why?

5. How might a sending congregation be helpful to your church?

Chapter 2

WHY SHOULD WE CONSIDER REPLANTING OUR CHURCH?

Now that you know there is hope for churches like yours, I want to share with you six reasons why I believe it is wise to at least consider the option of replanting your church. While replanting isn't the option available to a declining congregation, these are six reasons why replanting might just be the best strategy to help your congregation move into the future with renewed hope and gospel passion for the glory of God!

REASON #1: YOUR PEOPLE NEED ENCOURAGEMENT, NOURISHMENT, AND FRESH VISION.

First of all, my guess is that your people need encouragement. Typically when you step inside a declining church, you will quickly see folks who are tired. They're exhausted! They've probably lost passion and zeal. It's not that they desire to be dispassionate about the Lord, the church, or the lost. It's just that they've been going so hard for so long that they're simply worn out. Often, it's been a difficult season for that church, and likely the season has been a long one. Sound familiar? You surely know this more than anyone; your church needs encouragement—lots of loving encouragement!

Secondly, your people need nourishment. All of the Lord's sheep need nourishment. Sheep rely on receiving healthy food from a good shepherd, a pastor who faithfully preaches and teaches the Word of God. John 21:15 says, "When they had finished breakfast, Jesus said to Simon Peter, 'Simon, son of John, do you love me more than these?' He said to him, 'Yes, Lord; you know that I love you.' He said to him, 'Feed my lambs.'"

In the same way, it's the responsibility of a replanting pastor to feed God's flock good food for the renewing of their hearts and minds that they might move out on mission in their community with joy and strength in the Lord. Has it been a while since you've been spiritually fed this way? Declining congregations like yours need replanting pastors who can shepherd them well, nourishing them with the food of God's Word, while leading them with knowledge and understanding.

Thirdly, your people need fresh vision. Many times struggling churches have lost vision. As a result, they have lost hope and passion for what the Lord can do in and through their congregation. They need fresh vision and new hope. They need to be loved and led in such a way that they begin to believe the truth that God isn't done with their church. More than that, they need to believe that God is just getting started with what He wants to do in and through them for his purposes! This is true for your congregation as well.

REASON #2: THE LOST IN YOUR COMMUNITY NEED TO SEE JOYFUL, PASSIONATE, GOSPEL-CENTERED CONGREGATIONS ALIVE AND ON MISSION.

Many declining churches were at one time a central hub serving various needs in the community, reaching both children and adults with the good news of Jesus. However, over time and for various reasons, this has changed. These churches are no longer effectively reaching their communities, and they are probably trying to figure out why.

How desperately neighborhoods all across our country need these types of churches to be replanted and become lighthouses for Jesus once again! Can you imagine what this would look like for your church and community? What an exciting thing to think about! Replanted churches serve as a source of true hope, encouragement, love, and healing for people in their communities. The lost and the broken in these communities— communities just like yours—need the church, simply because they need Jesus.

REASON #3: YOUR CHURCH HAS BEEN CALLED TO MAKE DISCIPLES WHO MAKE DISCIPLES.

As his followers, Jesus has given us a clear mission. Our mission is to make disciples who make disciples. It is that straightforward. This is what we're called to do both as individuals and as congregations. Jesus is speaking to his disciples in Matthew 28:18-20, when we read these familiar words:

And Jesus came and said to them, "All authority in heaven and on earth has been given to me. Go therefore and make disciples of all nations, baptizing them in the name of the Father and of the Son and of the Holy Spirit, teaching them to observe all that I have commanded you. And behold, I am with you always, to the end of the age."

Jesus couldn't be more clear. The mission of the church is to make disciples of all nations, baptizing them and teaching them to obey all that he has commanded. While this great commission is short and to the point, does it seem like Jesus is asking too much? Thankfully, God is the One who saves, and he promises to be our strength and to be with us as we seek to follow his commands. This is another reason for you to consider being replanted as a congregation: to see the lost in your community being saved and discipled in the way of Jesus, that they might then go and disciple others. Simply put, more joyful and passionate disciples of Jesus will be made as churches like yours choose to be replanted for the glory of God.

REASON #4: THE GOD-HONORING STEWARDSHIP OF YOUR CHURCH'S MONEY, BUILDING, AND OTHER RESOURCES

What a privilege—yet big responsibility—it is for your church to steward the God-given resources that have been handed down throughout the history of your church. This is another reason why we need to become more serious about and passionate about replanting. Matt Schmucker, author and former executive director of 9Marks, writes:

> Billions of dollars, donated by faithful Christians over many decades, have been invested in land and buildings. Today, those buildings are too often underutilized or even empty—mere

monuments to the past...[we must] reclaim these resources that were originally given for gospel purposes.[1]

I think Matt is right-on here. The Lord has been honored in the past through faithful Christians in your church who have given generously to church building funds and other physical resources. We're called to be stewards of these generous past gifts as we seek to reach the surrounding community with the love of Christ. Replanting is one way to make sure these resources are stewarded well for Kingdom purposes.

REASON #5: YOUR CHURCH CAN BRING HOPE TO OTHER DYING CHURCHES AND TO THE BODY OF CHRIST AS A WHOLE.

I hope we would all agree that when we look at the New Testament, we see a constant theme of Christian encouragement. We are to encourage one another! We are to spur one another on, to build one another up. This is true not only as individuals but also as churches. If your church is in decline, you know more than anyone that you need encouragement right now. An exciting thing about the body is that when you receive encouragement, you can use it to encourage others. There is nothing more uplifting to a dying congregation than to see other declining congregations being replanted, transformed, and coming back to life.

What a joy it is to visit with many struggling churches and to share stories of the new life the Lord has brought to other congregations just like theirs through replanting. Hearing the stories, seeing pictures, and meeting the people of those replanted churches helps declining churches to see that there is hope for them! In turn, through replanting, your church has a unique opportunity to be a vessel of hope and encouragement to other churches that are hurting and in need of help. What a privilege to be used by God in this way—coming alongside other brothers and sisters in Christ, putting your arm around them and helping them to see that God is not done with their church either.

REASON #6: FOR THE PRAISE AND GLORY OF GOD'S NAME THROUGHOUT THE EARTH

This is the ultimate goal, the ultimate end in church replanting, because it is the ultimate goal and the ultimate end of all creation. The reason that God's glory must be our ultimate goal is because he alone is worthy of glory. God both desires and deserves to be glorified, and he has invited us to joyfully pursue the glory of his name in our lives and ministries. Of course, this includes the replanting of churches! There's probably no text in the Bible that reveals the passion that God has for his own glory more than what we see in Isaiah 48:9-11. This is where we read the Lord speaking,

> For my name's sake I defer my anger, for the sake of my praise I restrain it for you, that I may not cut you off. Behold, I have refined you, but not as silver; I have tried you in the furnace of affliction. For my own sake, for my own sake, I do it, for how should my name be profaned? My glory I will not give to another.

We're reminded in this text that the Lord has allowed many churches to struggle and go through difficult seasons, ultimately for his glory. But here's the reality: God, in his love, grace, and kindness, brings churches back from near death for his glory too. He desires servants, leaders, followers, and congregations who are humble enough to say, "Lord, this is all about you! This is not my church, this is Your church. This is the bride of Christ that Jesus died to save. Lord, be glorified in us. Be glorified in this church. For Your glory alone, Lord!" Along these lines, Matt Schmucker also writes:

> For the sake of God's name being rightly represented in the world, we need to be jealous for the witness of his church. Why? So that God's glory might be spread and magnified. His name is defamed when so-called Christian churches misrepresent him with tolerance of sin, their bad marriage practices, wrong views on sexuality, and a host of heresies from salvation to the authority of Scripture.
>
> I pray against those churches that would defame God's name. I pray they would die or at least be invisible to the neighborhood. I positively pray for those true churches in my neighborhood that proclaim truth, that rightly gather those who have been born again, and whose ultimate purpose is God's glory. Consider revitalizing for the sake of God's name.[2]

God is about his glory. We must be about his glory as well. The church can make a powerful impact, either positively or negatively. Mark Clifton, National Director of Replanting for the North American Mission Board (NAMB), has also written extensively on this very topic of replanting churches for the sake of God's fame and God's glory. He states:

> A dying church robs God of His Glory. The key to revitalization of a church near death is a passion for the Glory of God in all things. This alone must be the beginning and primary motivation for a Legacy replant, even over worthy objectives such as reaching the community, growing the church and meeting needs. The purpose of all creation is the glory of God. He created everything for His own glory.[3]

As Romans 11:36 proclaims, "For from him and through him and to him are all things. To him be glory forever. Amen."

Clifton is right; all things are to bring glory to the Lord. This remains true in church replanting. We want to see the glory of God spread to the ends of the earth as we see hopeless situations and dying churches redeemed for his fame. We want to see churches just like yours come back to life—even ones that outsiders (or insiders!) have looked at and said, "It's all over. There's no hope there." God has always been in the business of bringing dead things back to life, the best example being his own Son, Jesus. That's the gospel! In the same way, God is in the business of bringing dying churches back to life. his desire is the same in your church today. Praise the Lord for his life-giving work!

GOD **WASN'T** DONE WITH OUR CHURCH

Our church was like many established churches. It had been built to meet the growing city need for a local church facility that set itself apart as a central home. It has a traditional sanctuary with rooms split off on one end and in the basement an area for Sunday school, a kitchen to have potlucks and a wing to house the pre-school. Of course, age, use and funding have served to keep this look the same and maybe now it would be considered retro. But for those who have been there for most of its life, it's home.

There are just a few of us who have seen this old building when it really showed its age, a time where there were just a few of us still left thinking we would be the last. As our number shrank to the less than thirty, we were in a bit of a panic.

Our denomination's leadership at the time didn't give us any new ideas in what to do as we watched our church attendance dwindle and the facility fall further behind. At the time, the options, or at least we thought, were either to go with the next round of "available" pastor candidates or sell the building outright. We felt trapped in a loop of "recycled" candidates because our church just couldn't pay for a full-time pastor.

However, the option to sell just didn't ever feel right. Most of the remaining members left for more 'vibrant' churches, and the few families that stayed were either too old and set in their ways or just not ready to give up. We were all tired of the battles that exist in a dying church: the battle to keep the facility running, the battle to meet the needs of those who came through our doors, and the battle to see God's church not to be swallowed up by the neighborhood and its urban sprawl.

In this battle to stay faithful, older generations spoke up. They reminded us that this was God's church and that our church once reached this neighborhood for him and could again. But, this dream didn't seem to be his dream for us. Reality said that we were months from closing our doors. Our children were the only ones in Sunday School, and our pastors were either fill-ins, or (like the church itself) just barely hanging in there.

Maybe we were stubborn, but we knew that God loved our church and that he wanted to make himself known in our city. And without knowing it, we took the first step to revitalization, admitting that it was only him that could revive this dying church. We saw the need daily at our doors—people hungry for the gospel, hungry to be loved and cared for. We were a motley crew then, but God was showing us that we were still needed here, and that we needed him! Perhaps it was because we had no direction that it was easy to give in to his. We had to submit because we had nothing else left.

And we saw him show off his power to save. Just when it seemed our hope was gone, God provided anew. Reality said, "you're broke and your building is old and you have no direction and you are weary", but God had begun his work. He loves our little church just like he loves all of his people and desires to revitalize them. God is more faithful than we knew or thought or dared to dream.

Throughout this process, God was teaching us many things. First, we needed to submit to his leadership and lordship over us, before he would revive the dying. The church building is his, never ours. We are simply the laborers, and because the laborers are few, we need the Lord of the Harvest to tend the field.

That meant replanting our church's crops with new seeds, for we had lain fallow for far too long. We thought we were working the field, but we were just pulling weeds and watching them grow back. We "weed-pullers" would never harvest on our own. We need to let him harvest and those he ordained do the work.

Our church now isn't the church it once was. It definitely looks the same, but when we walk in those doors there is life. Today, our church is home to countless new families, a church where families start and where children grow in knowledge of God. Today, we are a body that hears the Bible, a body that is loved and hugged and fed. And, we are much different because of it.

When I open those doors to the sanctuary and hear all generations and all backgrounds lifting their voices in worship or see all the heads looking up at the teaching or down at their Bibles open wide, my heart rejoices in him and his faithfulness. One of the greatest joys for me is seeing all those children heading off to children's church with the noise filling those rooms again, knowing a generation is not lost. And I praise God to see the baptismal filled regularly, to hear the stories of his work in people from all walks of life, or to see people just walk up to the door because God's work cannot be ignored.

Many servants more faithful than us do not get to see revitalization. But by God's grace, we are still here, serving as best as we know how. He still calls us to be involved, and we are honored to be a part of those that came before as well as those who have come after. In fact, our family has been blessed to have had four generations walk in those doors on Sunday morning, not out of obligation, but out of a desire to hear His words preached. It isn't perfect. But, it was always his church, and he knows what is best for his bride.

- *Bart & Kim*

DISCUSSION QUESTIONS

1. What would it look like for your church to receive encouragement, nourishment, and fresh vision?

2. In what ways has your community benefited from your church in the past? What impact would you like to see your church make in your community now and in the future?

3. How can your church make disciples who make disciples?

4. In what ways can your church's money, building(s), and other resources be used to advance the Kingdom?

5. How can your church—currently and in the days ahead—encourage other declining churches and the body of Christ as a whole?

6. In what ways can your church bring glory to God?

Chapter 3

WHAT DOES GOD SAY ABOUT CHURCHES LIKE OURS?

God does some of his most remarkable work when things seem hopeless. He always has. This is true when it comes to working in the lives of individuals, and it is also true when it comes to working in the lives of dying churches. God's heart is for his church, including churches that are dying. When considering the topic of God's heart for replanting, there are four biblical convictions that are critical for us to hold. These are four biblical truths for you and your church to remember, embrace, and find hope in as you consider replanting your congregation.

CONVICTION #1: GOD DESIRES TO SEE DYING AND DECLINING CHURCHES COME BACK TO LIFE FOR HIS GLORY.

Without a doubt, God desires to see dying and declining churches come back to life. He's always looking for humble servants whom he can use for his purposes and bring glory to himself. We must become less so that he might become more. Here's the thing about the Lord: unlike most individuals in our fallen world who value strength, he uses and loves underdogs! Everywhere in the Scriptures, whether you're talking David and Goliath, or Jesus' disciples, or the Apostle Paul, the Lord always goes after and uses the "wrong" people. He chooses players on his team that you and I would never choose. He chooses the weak, the foolish, the uncool...and uses them in mighty ways!

This is the heart of God for both individuals and churches. God loves underdog churches. He loves it when the world is saying, "That church is dead and done. That church just needs to shut the doors." That's when God says, "You watch. I'm ready to do my best work right here, right now." The Lord is like that, and He's always been that way. Let's praise him for it!

One of the many things I love about God is that, in our weakness, he is strong. In 2 Corinthians, chapter 12, verses 9-10, the Apostle Paul writes this:

> But he said to me, "My grace is sufficient for you, for my power is made perfect in weakness." Therefore I will boast all the more gladly of my weaknesses, so that the power of Christ may rest upon me. For the sake of Christ, then, I am content with weaknesses, insults, hardships, persecutions, and calamities. For when I am weak, then I am strong.

This is key to every one of us as believers and leaders in Christ's Church: when we are weak, we are strong in the Lord. It's true for churches and congregations as well. When a church recognizes its weakness and brokenness, it is then in a place of humility where the Lord does his best work. It is in that place that God does the impossible. It is in that place that God makes a church strong again and brings it back to life for his glory.

Years ago, I came across a powerful quote from the great Baptist preacher Charles Spurgeon, and now I come back to it often. Concerning weakness and humility in ministry, Spurgeon writes:

> A primary qualification for serving God with any amount of success, and for doing God's work well and triumphantly, is a sense of our own weakness. When God's warrior marches forth to battle, strong in his own might, when he boasts, "I know that I shall conquer, my own right arm and my conquering sword shall get unto me the victory," defeat is not far distant. God will not go forth with that man who marches in his own strength. He who reckoneth on victory thus has reckoned wrongly, for "it is not by might, nor by power, but by my Spirit, saith the Lord of hosts." They who go forth to fight, boasting of their prowess, shall return with their banners trailed in the dust, and their armour stained with disgrace.[1]

What a great, yet convicting image. How often we seek to go forth in battle by our own strength. What foolishness! What pride! Spurgeon continues:

> Those who serve God must serve Him in His own way, and in His strength, or He will never accept their service. That which man doth, unaided by divine strength, God can never own. The mere fruits of the earth He casteth away; He will only reap that corn, the seed of which was sown from heaven, watered by grace, and ripened by the sun of divine love. God will empty out all that thou hast before He will put His own into thee; He will first clean out thy granaries before He will fill them with the finest of the wheat.[2]

In other words, until we recognize our emptiness and weakness, he won't fill us with the power of his Spirit. And if you're like me, I not only want, but I know I need, his power. I need his power more than anything in my life and ministry.

With this in mind, consider this last quote from Spurgeon on the topic of God's strength and our weakness:

> The river of God is full of water; but not one drop of it flows from earthly springs. God will have no strength used in His battles but the strength which He Himself imparts.
>
> Are you mourning over your own weakness? Take courage, for there must be a consciousness of weakness before the Lord will give thee victory. Your emptiness is but the preparation for your being filled, and your casting down is but the making ready for your lifting up.[3]

Such wise and truth-filled words for each of us! With those in mind, let me offer two simple but important points of application, the first being personal for each of us. As leaders in the church, we must understand and embrace this truth: Until we empty ourselves, humbling ourselves before the Lord, he will not do what he wants to do in us and through us. The Lord doesn't need us; he doesn't need anything. But, it is his delight to use us and invite us into his work of ministry and mission in the world.

A second application is for dying and declining churches. Until a congregation humbles itself and recognizes its need, this church should not expect the Lord to pour out his Spirit and bring dead bones back to life. He is looking for a humble and dependent people who seek to make a big deal about him as they joyfully submit to his Word and his Will. Remember, both in our personal lives and in our churches, God loves to give strength to the needy, to those who are desperate for him. Will we be those kinds of people? Those kinds of churches?

Look at the words of Jesus in John 7:37-39:

> On the last day of the feast, the great day, Jesus stood up and cried out, "If anyone thirsts, let him come to me and drink. Whoever

believes in me, as the Scripture has said, 'Out of his heart will flow rivers of living water.'" Now this he said about the Spirit, whom those who believed in him were to receive, for as yet the Spirit had not been given, because Jesus was not yet glorified.

Jesus is pointing to the indwelling power of the Holy Spirit we desperately need as individuals, leaders, and churches. I often pray that the church I serve will be filled with the Holy Spirit of God and that lives would be changed: that many would be saved by the Spirit; that marriages would be restored; that children, at a young age, would come to a saving faith in Christ. This is what I desire to see in our church, and the Spirit of God desires to see this far more than I do. He always has. But it begins with us, as his people, humbling ourselves in faith, asking and believing that the Lord can do these things according to his perfect will. It begins with each of us on our knees, praying with David in Psalm 51:10–12,

> "Create in me a clean heart, O God, and renew a right spirit within me. Cast me not away from your presence, and take not your Holy Spirit from me. Restore to me the joy of your salvation, and uphold me with a willing spirit."

May this prayer be the cry of our hearts both as individuals and as churches. The hard truth is this: Any church that cannot pray the prayer, "Oh, God, create in us a clean heart, renew us, revive us, humble us," is too prideful and too hardhearted. If they can't pray that prayer, that church should not expect God to do miraculous things and bring that church back to life. Our posture must always be one of humility before the Lord.

CONVICTION #2: GOD HAS BOTH THE DESIRE AND THE POWER TO BRING DYING AND DECLINING CHURCHES BACK TO LIFE FOR HIS GLORY.

I hope you believe this. When it comes to replanting dying churches, God isn't sitting there wringing his hands and saying, "Oh boy, I sure wish that kind of thing could happen, but I really don't have the power to do anything about it." No, the Lord is the all-powerful, sovereign King of the universe. He not only has the desire, but he also has the power to bring anything that is dead back to life, including a local church.

Ezekiel 37 is a great picture of the Lord bringing something dead back to life. At this point in the text, both Jerusalem and the temple have been destroyed. Judgment has come. But God reveals himself in this passage as a God of revitalization, as a God of resurrection.

In Ezekiel 37:1-6, we read this:

> The hand of the LORD was upon me, and he brought me out in the Spirit of the LORD and set me down in the middle of the valley; it was full of bones. And he led me around among them, and behold, there were very many on the surface of the valley, and behold, they were very dry. And he said to me, "Son of man, can these bones live?" And I answered, "O Lord GOD, you know." Then he said to me, "Prophesy over these bones, and say to them, O dry bones, hear the word of the LORD. Thus says the Lord GOD to these bones: Behold, I will cause breath to enter you, and you shall live. And I will lay sinews upon you, and will cause flesh to come upon you, and cover you with skin, and put breath in you, and you shall live, and you shall know that I am the LORD."

Only our God can do something as powerful and miraculous as bringing dead, dry bones back to life! He does this very thing with us as individuals, and he does it with churches.

There are two essential ingredients for God-honoring replanting and true revitalization in the church that I want to point out from this passage:

Ingredient#1: The Faithful Preaching of God's Word

In his excellent book *Can These Dry Bones Live?*, Bill Henard writes:

> The first requirement necessitates the preaching of God's Word. God tells Ezekiel, "Prophesy concerning those bones" (37:4). As Ezekiel obeys, the Scripture unveils this magnificent vision of bones taking on tendons and flesh. Note carefully that the bones described are dry bones. These soldiers who died in battle were not afforded the privilege of a proper burial. They experienced the great disgrace of open decay. Yet God intervenes, and Ezekiel speaks to the bones.[4]

What an image as we think about church replanting and revitalization! The preaching of God's Word has the power to bring dry bones, souls, and churches back to life. It is living and active as we preach, counsel with, and share the Word with folks in church sanctuaries and over coffee and meals.

Ingredient #2: The Presence and Power of the Holy Spirit

Again, Henard writes:

> In order for the church to be revived (to be revitalized, to experience new life, new health, new growth), it will demand a mighty work of God's Spirit. Following a particular methodology or program does not guarantee success. One might greatly desire for the church to revitalize and grow, but genuine church growth calls for more than personal passion. It requires the Spirit of God.[5]

That is the truth! We can read all the books we want. We can come up with the most dynamic, exciting, fresh, and compelling strategies the world of church revitalization and church replanting has ever seen, but without the Spirit of God moving, dead bones don't come back to life. They just don't. Church replanting begins with laying the foundation of God's Word as it is preached and as the congregation is empowered by a profound movement of God's Spirit.

CONVICTION #3: TRUE CHURCH REVITALIZATION WILL NOT HAPPEN UNLESS A CONGREGATION RETURNS TO THEIR FIRST LOVE–JESUS.

Dry bones won't come back to life and churches won't be revitalized unless a church returns to its first love, which is Jesus Christ. In Revelation 2:1-3, we read words that may be familiar to many of us in the church. In this passage, the Lord is speaking to the church at Ephesus:

> To the angel of the church in Ephesus write: "The words of him who holds the seven stars in his right hand, who walks among the seven golden lampstands. I know your works, your toil and your patient endurance, and how you cannot bear with those who are evil, but have tested those who call themselves apostles and are not, and found them to be false. I know you are enduring patiently and bearing up for my name's sake, and you have not grown weary."

This is a great church! This is a church that is steady and faithful. This is a church that has endured much, all the while remaining steadfast in the Lord. This is a congregation that is rock solid when it comes to understanding sound doctrine. This is a church that loves the Bible. There is much to be commended in this church. But notice what Jesus says next, in verses 4 and 5:

"But I have this against you, that you have abandoned the love you had at first. Remember therefore from where you have fallen; repent, and do the works you did at first. If not, I will come to you and remove your lampstand from its place, unless you repent."

The picture here is of a church that has its doctrine right, and its missions giving is probably greater than any other in its local church association. It's doing all kinds of things right. Yet when Jesus looks at the heart of this church, he sees a people who is no longer in love with him. They may say and think they are, but they aren't really. Their passion for Christ has dwindled. There's no zeal for the things of God. The study of God's Word has become simply an academic exercise. The Word is no longer setting the heart of this church on fire for evangelism and missions—its head perhaps, but not its heart. And so the Lord says, "If you don't return to your first love, if you don't do those things you did at first when you had a simple, childlike faith in me and love for me, unless you repent and turn back to me, I'm going to take your lampstand away."

Mark Clifton says that in this passage, the Lord makes it clear that the pathway to new life for a dying church is repentance and remembering. Those are two key words for any church that wants to be revitalized—repent and remember. But Clifton clarifies what this type of remembering means exactly:

...not the self-serving nostalgia of remembering the past for the sake of our own edification through control and a desire to return to a "better time," but remembering the legacy of missions and ministry that first birthed this dying church and a brokenness to see that return once again. This kind of remembering can only happen if repentance comes first. This kind of remembering can only happen when the Glory of God becomes primary rather than the glory of the past.[6]

There's one main reason why a church dies: It has lost its first love. For the members of a declining church, this is heartbreaking to hear. Of course they love Jesus and always mean to put him first. But perhaps a heart check is still in order. Perhaps they have done many things in the name of Jesus that became less about him and his kingdom and slowly brought the mission off track. It is when we lose our first love that we begin to lose everything. We lose our love for the truth, and we lose our love for the lost. When we lose our love for the Lord and the things of the Lord, we increase our love for self and our own "kingdom" rather than God's. And so we must beg God in all humility, "Oh Lord, change our hearts. Turn our hearts back toward you, that you would be the love and passion of our lives. Lord, may you be our greatest treasure in this life and forevermore!"

CONVICTION #4: WHEN A CHURCH RETURNS TO ITS FIRST LOVE, JESUS, GOD BEGINS TO BRING ABOUT REVITALIZATION THROUGH THREE TYPES OF RENEWAL.

When a church comes to the point of genuine humility, returning to Jesus and the gospel as its first love, then and only then does God begin to bring about true renewal and revitalization. He does this through three types of renewal.[7]

#1: Personal Renewal

When a dying congregation's leaders experience personal renewal, true congregational renewal begins. This starts with the hearts of the leaders. Personal renewal means that leaders in the church recognize the need for more of the Holy Spirit.

These leaders begin to grow in humility, in love for people, and in love for the lost. As leaders, we cannot take people where we've never been. We cannot give what we do not have. This is why congregational renewal begins with personal renewal. And this is why our love for the Lord and his Word must be primary.

#2: Relational Renewal

In a church where leaders begin to experience personal renewal, relational renewal should naturally begin to follow. Relational renewal means that leaders are not only right with God, but they are also getting right with others. The leaders in a congregation are doing all they can to pursue peace, unity, and harmony with others in the congregation. Reconciliation marked by genuine kindness and love for other brothers and sisters in Christ should be a top priority. Pastor Rick Warren says this:

> When you have relational renewal in your church, the gossip goes down and the joy goes up. How do you know when a church has been through relational renewal? People hang around longer after the service. They want to spend time together. If people don't want to hang around after your services, you have a performance, not a church. The church is more than content; it's a community.[8]

#3: Missional Renewal

As leaders grow in their love for God and he begins to renew their hearts, it spreads out to others and results in relational renewal. This then begins to lead a congregation outside the walls of the church on mission. It's inevitable—if the Spirit of God renews us, the Spirit of God is going to align our desires with God's desires. This looks like living life on mission, seeking to reach those in the community with the good news of the gospel.

This type of missional renewal is seen not only in the leadership, but will also spread through the congregation as individuals and families grow in their passion and conviction to make disciples of Jesus. When missional renewal begins to happen, a church begins to believe they need to reach the lost and are willing to do whatever it takes to do it. It is when a church begins to experience this third type of renewal that God begins to do incredible things in a dying church. This is when replanting gets really fun! What a joy to see a church get back on mission, no longer focusing on itself and its survival but on the lost and the surrounding community that deeply needs Jesus. This is God's desire for dying churches. This is God's heart for replanting.

God loves his church. He loves his people. He loves to bring dead bones back to life. In this way, his heart is to breathe new life into struggling congregations for the salvation of the lost, for the joy of his people, and for the spread of his fame throughout the earth. From the world's perspective, there seems to be little hope for dying churches. However, when we see the heart of God in his Word, we have much reason for hope—that God will do what only he can do: breathe new life into the dry, dusty bones of churches all over the world for his glory. This includes your church too!

GOD **WASN'T** DONE WITH OUR CHURCH

When we first attended our church, over 10 years ago, we had been "church-homeless" for over a year. We left our longtime, previous church home out of necessity, and after visiting several churches, working through a painful season of healing, the Lord providentially brought us to our current one. And, unbeknownst to us, it was a time of big transition!

Our experience at the church that Sunday morning was one of comfortably full pews, the singing of old hymns and friendly folks, and we had a sense that this might be the place we had long sought for, a place where we could grow roots once again. Little did we know that the pastor was on his way out, and the bulk of the congregation would follow him out the door.

Without leadership, the church quickly shrunk to a handful of faithful folks, a remnant no doubt placed there by the Lord with purpose. We knew that the Lord had led us to this church, but it became an arduous journey together, calling a new pastor only to have him leave a short time later while finances quickly dwindled. We certainly questioned what the Lord was up to and why he had brought us to this "dying" church. Still, fellowship with the few who remained was genuine and sweet and we trusted that he was at work.

Once again, another search committee was formed and began gathering candidates' names, when the Lord intervened. He gave us the pastor whom he had prepared for our church for this very time. He gave us a man with a dream, a vision, and a passion, first for the Lord and secondly for the community!

We cannot say for sure if our church even thought of revitalization, but that is what the Lord provided. The Lord intended to work through this small group of folks, to move them to seek him without holding to tradition or agenda, and to keep the doors open while he breathed fresh life, REVITALIZATION, into our church and into our community, making us a vibrant, healthy community of faith!

From a well-sized congregation, to a fainting few, to a now growing and thriving body—it is a privilege to share the Lord's faithfulness in and through the revitalization of our church. We would not want to suggest that size alone is always a true indicator of health and growth in a church, yet the Holy Spirit has used our church to now draw many from this community, hungry for truth, into relationship with God.

We have seen his hand in countless ways as we have continued to trust him to show us how to "do church". He is on his throne, Sovereign and ready to move into our broken and humble spaces, particularly as we lay down our agendas and seek him first for the salvation of the lost, the building of his kingdom, and the praise of his Great Glory!

- Kenny & Sue

DISCUSSION QUESTIONS

1. How would you describe God's heart for church replanting?

2. Take time to think about God's glory. Why is it such a big deal?

3. What does true humility, weakness, and brokenness look like in ministry and day-to-day life?

4. Discuss how the Lord's business of bringing the dead to life could demonstrate the gospel (the Good News of Jesus) for a church replant.

5. Do you believe God has both the desire and the power to bring dying and declining churches back to life? How could this belief change your prayer life?

6. What is your reaction toward the idea that declining congregations have lost their first love, Jesus?

7. Can you think of examples in your own church in which the mission might have strayed away from a complete dependence and focus on Christ?

8. What does a church which holds firm to their first love, Jesus, look like?

Chapter 4

WHAT ARE THE COSTS & JOYS OF REPLANTING?

"There is a cost to this, boys!"

I remember these words from one of my basketball coaches when I was younger. "If you boys wanna be great basketball players…if you wanna be a great team…if you wanna win a bunch of games…if you wanna be champions……there is a cost to this, boys! There is a cost to this!"

Of course, my coach was right. To have success on the basketball court, as with every other area of life, it takes blood, sweat, and tears. It doesn't just happen; it takes effort, hard work, and discipline. Because of this, we always need to count the cost of anything we do—physically, spiritually, mentally, and emotionally.

When considering all that goes into replanting a congregation like yours, we have to be honest about the real challenges that will potentially come. As with other areas of life and ministry, Jesus calls us to count the cost. In Luke 14:27–33, we see Jesus laying out the cost of following him, the cost of being his disciple. He says:

Whoever does not bear his own cross and come after me cannot be my disciple. For which of you desiring to build a tower does not first sit down and count the cost, whether he has enough to complete it? Otherwise, when he has laid a foundation and is not able to finish, all who see it begin to mock him, saying, 'This man began to build and was not able to finish.' Or what king, going out to encounter another king in war, will not sit down first and deliberate whether he is able with ten thousand to meet him who comes against him with twenty thousand? And if not, while the other is yet a great way off, he sends a delegation and asks for terms of peace. So therefore, any one of you who does not renounce all that he has cannot be my disciple.

Jesus is giving us examples of building a tower and going to war as illustrations of the wisdom that comes through counting the cost in advance. Specifically, he is talking about counting the cost of being his disciple. This passage is relevant not only to counting the cost in following Jesus, but in counting the cost of church replanting. Jesus is asking us if we are up for the challenges that come in helping to lead a declining church back to life.

At the same time, we must also be honest about the real opportunities that potentially lie ahead in replanting as well—there is great joy that comes in replanting a church! There are few things more exciting than being part of a congregation that was dying and then seeing the Holy Spirit bring that church back to life. In this chapter, I want to help you consider several real challenges as well as several real opportunities that lie ahead as you consider both the cost and joy of church replanting.

THE CHALLENGES OF REPLANTING

Let's begin by considering several potential challenges as we begin to count the cost of church replanting. Whether you consider your church to be dying, declining, or just "not what it used to be," you have to admit that probably more than one thing has gone wrong in the process. The following points are not meant to make you feel guilty or overwhelmed, but hopefully they will help you more readily "go with the flow" of inevitable changes that need to be made, as well as fight against repeating the same mistakes.

Challenge #1: Culture Change

In replanting, leaders are called to lovingly and wisely help change a church culture. Leaders are trying to create change in the midst of an existing culture that is not as healthy as it once was. The primary challenge in changing culture is simply this: It takes time. It takes time to earn trust, and it takes time to display Christ-like patience when some in the congregation would like to make changes, but others aren't yet ready.

In this regard, effective church replanting is much more like a marathon than a sprint. Changing culture is a long haul, a steady run. It is a constant abiding in Jesus, loving the people of God, living on mission, preaching the Word, serving the community, praying hard for the flock and the lost—over and over again. These are means God uses to bring declining churches back to life, but of course it all takes time.

Challenge #2: Hidden Sacred Cows

With this in mind, it's key for churches to be willing to recognize and examine hang-ups that might've been held onto too tightly for too long. Every existing church has sacred cows—it's just the truth. A sacred cow is an idea, custom, or tradition that is almost immune from questioning in a church and often unreasonably so. Sacred cows in churches are often above critique or criticism of any kind.

More often than not, dying churches have multiple sacred cows that can be like land mines—you usually don't know that they're even there until you've already stepped on it. It may be changing the music style or putting up new artwork on the walls. It could be replacing the pews with chairs or beginning to project song lyrics onto a screen rather than using hymnals. Whatever it might be, stepping on these land mines can create major division and cause a church to lose focus on what is most important, namely, Jesus and the gospel. Mark Clifton is correct when he writes:

Dying churches tend to make their preferences paramount. Those preferences can include music, programs, preaching styles, uses of the building, resources shared with those outside the church compared to resources used for those within the church, and a host of other things. The point is this: Most members of the congregation focus on their own desires in these decisions instead of what would meet the needs of people who don't know Jesus.[1]

For every one of us, this is our unfortunate tendency over time—to take our eyes off meeting the needs of others and to be more concerned about the needs of ourselves. Sacred cows are often the fruit of this. It is a very real challenge that takes much wisdom, courage, grace, and humility to lead through in church replanting.

Challenge #3: Lack of Desire to Reach the Lost

Every church that claims to love Jesus, love the gospel, and love the Word will say that they want to grow. They will say they want to reach the lost. Every church will say that they want to reach young people, children, young families, and those far from Jesus. Even dying churches will say this. Of course! That's why we have church, right? But the question is, in the heart of hearts of many folks in that congregation, do they really want this? Do they really want to do whatever it takes to make disciples of Christ? If they've gotten off track, it might seem like too much work and even unnecessary to make the changes that would put them back on mission. The hard truth is that all too often, few churchgoers are really willing to put personal preferences aside and do what it takes.

As hard as it is to acknowledge, this is something we need to name as a reality. Many churches are unwilling to put preferences aside for the sake of the broken, hurting, and lost. In my experience working with declining churches, many congregations can say the right things in terms of wanting to be revitalized, wanting a fresh start to reach the lost. But when the rubber hits the road, there are often key leaders in these churches who say, "I don't actually want that. I want to reach people without having to make the changes you are talking about. If replanting means our church has to change (this or that), then we're not in."

Pastor and author Mike McKinley says this:

> There's usually a good reason why a church needs to be revitalized. Churches often dwindle in size and effectiveness because of a traumatic event or years of poor leadership. As a result, church facilities and programs may be in ruins—not to mention the spiritual state of the congregation itself. In these cases, there will be much to overcome and tear down in order to move the church forward. This process is often very painful. If a church was already inclined to do the things that healthy churches do, it probably wouldn't be dying. Finding a struggling church isn't a problem. Finding a struggling church that wants to change and grow is much more difficult.[2]

Challenge #4: Lack of Love for the Surrounding Community

This can be another major challenge in replanting—helping the people who have been a part of this church for many years fall in love with their surrounding, changing community. It's hard to admit, but many churches in need of replanting have lost touch with their communities. The reason for this, in many cases, is that over the years the members have taken great care and pride in the physical building, without caring just as much for the community in which the building finds itself. The building becomes an idol, which then lends itself to an inward or misguided focus.

A fancy building, contrary to popular belief, will not tell the community that they are "here to stay." A full parking lot each week as well as happy neighbors will tell that story. The building is a great tool—praise God! But the community doesn't care about the building. The community cares about the love that those inside that building are expressing. Whether due to fear, laziness, apathy, sole focus on those already within their walls, or lack of intentional strategy, these churches are not shining as brightly as they could for Christ and the gospel in their community.

This is one of the greatest leadership challenges in replanting—helping a dying congregation fall in love again with the surrounding community in such a way that their hearts begin to break for those who do not know Jesus. Does your heart break for the community surrounding your church?

Challenge #5: Lack of Spiritual Health and Vibrancy

While some in the congregation may be healthy and growing in their walk with the Lord, this typically will not be the norm in declining churches. Many congregants are stagnant. Many are dry. Many have become discouraged, but it isn't necessarily their fault. As was discussed in Chapter 2, they have not been under good shepherding. It's very likely that they have not been pastored well for a long time. They haven't eaten good spiritual food from the Word of God. As a result, they are tired, and they are hungry. They need to be encouraged. They need to be fed.

But this is a real challenge in replanting. This is not a congregation in which folks are spiritually alive and fired up, ready to go live on mission. Folks here are tired and beat up and worn out. They need a lot of care and love. They need prayer and good food from the Word. You know this personally! Helping the congregation grow spiritually must be a top priority in replanting.

Challenge #6: Reliance on Programs or Personalities

It is very common for a declining church to believe that all they need to do to get healthy and begin growing again is a new cutting-edge program, or a new dynamic young pastor, or a new magnetic youth pastor. The mindset is this: "If we can just get that program, pastor, or youth pastor in here, we will start reaching young families again. Everything will surely get turned around!" Of course, that's not true at all. Young families won't save a church—only Jesus can! One leader cannot turn a declining church around. One program cannot do it. There's no magic bullet in church revitalization. Because of this, there often is an overabundance of purposeless programs and activities that have been tried throughout the years. Mark Clifton writes:

> Declining churches reach for programs and personalities they believe will turn the church around without embracing the changes needed to become healthy again. And it's hard to blame them for this predisposition since many past church-growth methodologies relied heavily on both. No doubt, as a dying church reflects on its heyday of growth, they recall a particular pastor or two who, by sheer force of personal charisma and leadership, moved the church to a new level. Or they recall a program or series of programs that once attracted all ages of people to become involved in the life of the church. With that history in mind, dying churches often think that applying programs and hiring personalities will be easy fixes to their problems. They quickly discover that neither fixes anything. In fact, their desire for a "silver bullet" program or personality reinforces their belief that they don't have to make major changes or repent of past mistakes or sacrifice their preferences for the needs of the unchurched, but they just have to add one more program or hire one more professional to fix the problem. In essence they are still trying to use primarily attractional methods in a community that no longer responds to those methods. It is frustrating and confusing for a dying church to accept that what worked so well in the past may in fact be hastening its demise.[3]

As painful as it might be to hear, Clifton is spot on. Despite all of the hard work and good intentions that have gone into such programs and activities, they weren't what the church needed after all. This magic-bullet mindset of the program or personality is something of which we need to be aware as we consider the leadership challenges in replanting.

Challenge #7: A Large, Unmanaged Membership Roll

One mark of a healthy, growing church is that it has more visitors and attenders showing up weekly to Sunday morning worship than it does church members. There are many reasons why this is true, and it communicates a lot of things. For instance, it demonstrates that there's a standard for membership. That church membership matters. That there are expectations and requirements for membership. That the folks who are members of this congregation are committed, devoted, and all in.

On the other hand, one of the marks of an unhealthy church is that the reverse happens; there are far more members of the congregation than there are visitors and attenders showing up in worship. It's not uncommon for churches to have three or four hundred members on the books while, at the same time, they only have thirty to forty in worship on a typical Sunday. This clearly is not healthy. So what should be done about it?

Simply put, what this means is that the membership rolls need to be updated and cleaned up. There needs to be an honest evaluation considering what membership really means in this church. What are they expecting of their members? Are their expectations clear to everyone? Are they following through on these expectations? Questions like these are especially important in churches where congregational members are actively involved in matters of decision making and voting. The church makes sure that members have skin in the game. A healthy church will ensure that those who have voting privileges are actively engaged in church ministry and are on board with the vision and direction of the congregation.

It is all too common to hear horror stories of churches in which a major vote needs to happen to bring on a new staff member or adjust the budget, only to be held hostage by "members" who are completely disengaged from the ministry and fellowship of the congregation. While there are a small but potent number of active members in regular worship and other church activities and programs, at that congregational meeting, thirty to forty other members who haven't been there perhaps in years, show up and sway the vote, sadly hindering the mission of that church. For this scenario—and so many like it— updating the membership rolls is absolutely critical. This can be another major challenge in replanting.

THE ADVANTANGES OF REPLANTING

We have considered several potential challenges that must be considered when counting the cost of church replanting. Let's now consider some of the potential advantages and unique opportunities that await when replanting. Each of these are catalysts for great joy in this important ministry.

Advantage #1: A New, Exciting, Positive Witness in the Community

Healthy, biblical church replanting establishes a new and fresh gospel presence in a community. If healthy churches make a positive statement about the gospel to the surrounding community (and they do), dying churches can often send a negative one, whether they realize it or not. What does it say to a community when a church dies? It says about this Jesus stuff, "Eh, I could take it or leave it. I mean, where's the power in this Jesus, in this gospel that they proclaim? They can't even keep their doors open."

The thought of this burdens me like no other. I hope it burdens you as well. On the flip side of this, when a community sees a dying church come back to life, that watching community sees a fresh, real, dynamic witness for Jesus where formerly there was an anti-witness.

Here's what we know. Wherever that declining church is located, it is surrounded by a community filled with people who don't know Jesus. I don't care if you're talking California or Texas or Alabama or New York or Colorado or Swaziland! Wherever that church is, I promise you, it is surrounded by people who don't know Jesus and are in desperate need of the gospel. Of course, this includes your church.

This is a huge opportunity that comes with church replanting. We get to see God do what only he can do: bring a dying church back to life for his glory as the lost are saved through the person and work of Jesus Christ. In doing this, the Lord exchanges a negative church witness with a positive one in a community. The fame of Jesus spreads as a result.

Advantage #2: A Building

You have a church building! Not every church can say that. This is a true gift. When you have your own building, you can do all kinds of creative ministry. Many church planters have shared with me the ongoing challenges of having to set up and take down chairs and tables and signs, week in and week out, in their auditorium or school meeting area. Church planters know all too well how tiresome it can be on staff and volunteers to not have a permanent location where the space is their own.

You are blessed with a building! As a result, you can use your building for all kinds of purposes beyond just Sunday morning. Your building can be a tool for outreach of various kinds, to kids and youth, to the homeless, to the community at large. There can be Bible studies, community groups, after-school clubs. You have a building! Having a building allows a church to make a huge statement to a community that says, "We are here. We love this community. We love Jesus. We want to help and serve in his name! This building is the Lord's to be used to bless the people of this community!" There's nothing like a congregation being embedded in a particular community for the sake of the gospel. A building helps churches like yours do this well for the long haul.

Advantage #3: Older Christians

Most declining churches have had a very difficult time reaching younger people and younger families. What you usually find in these congregations are older saints who have been faithful for a long time, working hard to hold things together. Some might see this as a negative. I believe it is a big plus! The Church is at its healthiest when it is intergenerational. This is true and biblical. The presence of older Christians is a major ingredient to a truly healthy, vibrant, biblical congregation. Let me share three of the many gifts that older saints bring to a church replant:

#1. Older Christians have maturity and experience.

Older saints have maturity and experience in life and in following Jesus that younger people simply don't have. With that maturity and experience comes wisdom that younger folks desperately need. I get so excited when I see churches that have a vision for this, of combining and connecting older generations with the younger for the sake of mutual edification and encouragement.

#2. Older Christians often have time and availability.

Younger people, younger couples, younger families are busy as can be. They just are. They're going a million miles an hour with school, sports, and all kinds of other activities and commitments. Many older saints have more time and availability. Many are retired, and their kids have been out of the house for a long time. As a result, they can serve in various ways younger people simply cannot. They have time to give, and the whole congregation is blessed by them as a result.

#3. Older Christians have skills, gifts, and passions.

Older folks have skills, gifts, and passions given to them by the Lord. But, sadly, so many times these individuals are underutilized and underdeveloped in our churches. Encouraging and equipping our older saints to lean into these gifts is a beautiful thing. It is a God-glorifying thing. We have an opportunity through church replanting to engage and unleash older generations in a unique way for the Kingdom. We can help them finish their race strong, encouraging them to serve the Lord faithfully and to reach others with the gospel to the very end. What a joy this is!

Advantage #4: Resources, Resources, Resources!

Another big opportunity that comes from churches being replanted is that their resources can be used for Kingdom work. Churches that are declining typically have some resources. Even if the resources are limited, they still have something that can be used for gospel ministry. This is a huge plus. It would be tragic to see these churches fall to ruin. Mike McKinley pointedly and accurately describes this reality:

> Many dead churches are sitting on a treasure trove of resources (land, money, equipment) that can be leveraged for the spread of the gospel. Those resources are just sitting around idle, doing almost nothing for the kingdom. As a matter of good stewardship, evangelical churches interested in planting should consider revitalizing as well. And let's be honest, if we don't revitalize these churches, they will most likely fall into the hands of liberal churches, mosques, or condominium developers.[4]

Advantage #5: History and Tradition

Some view the history and tradition of a church as solely a bad thing. And while history can be a potential negative in certain contexts, I believe it to be much more of a positive in most cases. I was with a group of pastors and denominational leaders not long ago, and as we were talking about some of the challenges involved in replanting, one of the men who was there piped up and gave a fairly brutal indictment against the whole idea of church replanting and revitalization. He looked at the group and said, "I don't get it. I really don't. This replanting thing is just crazy. I don't know how anybody could do that. It seems like a suicide mission." He went on, "You know, replanting sounds to me like trying to plant a church but with a whole bunch of baggage that you've got to deal with. Why would anyone choose to do that?" He was very sincere in asking this question. He could not fathom why anyone would want to pursue a ministry like this.

At that moment, a young man pursuing replanting ministry corrected this church leader and his flawed perspective. He looked at him and said, "Baggage is not what you are dealing with in replanting. History is what you're dealing with. A very precious history where God has been at work in major ways through the life of this congregation."

What this young replanter understood is that when you have a pastor's heart, and you love people well and understand that God has been at work in a declining church for many years, one begins to lean in and see the beauty of the history and the tradition of a congregation. Your church has a history and tradition where God has been—and still is—at work. This is a history that, by God's grace, you have been invited into. It is a sacred privilege to be part of this story the Lord has been writing for many years.

Advantage #5: Redemption of a Church for God's Glory

The last potential advantage I want you to consider is this— ultimately the great joy of church replanting is that we get to see God glorified (We could never exhaust the topic of God's glory!). We get to see God glorified as He redeems and restores churches that many people have given up on—churches that are not powerful or influential in the eyes of the world. Let us remember, the Lord loves to take weakness and show off his glory and his strength in bringing dead and dying things back to life.

That's the story of the gospel! This is the story we want to tell over and over again. The story of the gospel is that we were dead, and Christ came and made us alive. We are new creations! And this gospel story is so beautifully seen and told in the replanting of churches—the replanting of churches just like yours.

GOD **WASN'T** DONE WITH OUR CHURCH

I came to our church when I was in the ninth grade, and there I met my wife of 50 years, Nancy. Our entire life has been spent here. When we started attending, it was newly established, popular and well-attended, including many of our peers from the Junior High across the street. The meetings were always packed, and many times we brought in chairs to line the aisles with so people could sit. From the beginning, our church had a heart to start new churches in Colorado.

Over the years if you had to describe the people here the word people would use is 'love'. Our first daughter was born with severe special needs, and without asking, our church surrounded our family with support, encouragement, and love that lasted her entire lifetime. They helped raise not only our other 3 children, but our foster children and thousands more over the years. People who have been gone for years still come to visit our church just because they remember the love that poured from the people there.

Yet, our church often seemed to have power struggles, and at times, people did not seem to seek God's leadership when decisions were made. As a result, many Pastors have come and gone, yet we knew God is still at work. Even though the number of people grew smaller, we never felt like numbers were important and that in God's time growth would come. We felt people would come who truly loved him and would want to reach lost souls for Christ.

It never really occurred to us that we would have to shut the doors, and we could not understand others that thought we should. We had always felt God's presence and leadership, and there were many people living around our church that needed to hear about Jesus. We knew God was not through with Calvary, but we were waiting on his perfect timing.

We have come to love every pastor God has brought to our church because we have learned so much from each one. Each one stretched our church in different ways and is part of our legacy. And along the way, we learned we needed to stop having a church that was comfortable to us.

We agreed to seek real leadership next, not just someone to fill the pulpit. And when, our children told us, "You guys have had your day and now it is our turn to worship joyfully," we began to pray in a different way. God showed us that we needed to be more joyful in our approach to worship, to not be afraid to embrace change or ideas that were different than what we had done in the past.

Nancy was on our search team that brought the next pastor to our church. I had not met him but I will never forget my first encounter. I went into the auditorium to talk with one of our deacons, and this guy was in there with him. I had not seen this guy, but he reached over and gave me a big bear hug. He said he knew me and he loved me. And, he meant it. I do not know the last time I had hugged anyone in church, but I knew this was the man God had called to teach us how to worship joyfully and truly love others.

Our pastor brought a love for others that I had not seen in a pastor. He told us, all 30 members, to care for our neighbors around the church and to bring an offering of food for them when we came next Sunday. And so, we reached out to those in need and told them to come with no strings attached, just love. They did not have to attend or accept Christ, just come and let us love you.

Soon, people started coming. The word started to spread, and people just showed up asking what was going on, wanting to be a part of this movement, too. We stood in awe at what the Holy Spirit was doing with this little church. We were amazed that people would want to come to this old building to worship. And, worship they did! They came to worship a holy God who is full of love and compassion.

People with every kind of hang up found they could come here and be loved without the judgement. Our pastor showed us not to worry about people changing, but to simply love them and leave the change to God. People fear change and do not accept it willingly, but it comes easy, when we embrace change to glorify God.

Growing did not come without problems. Our supplies had to be doubled and then tripled. Our facilities not only had to be cleaned up but changed. We had to remodel and try to plan for the growth. Again, God used this time of work to build relationships. Even people I had just met were willing to help like they had gone there forever, cleaning, building, and serving without recognition because they love God's church.

God has allowed me to be a part of an exhilarating time. Every time I come into our church, I am still amazed at what God can do if we get out of the way. Early on, I (Dave) remember praying with our pastor that we would not get in the way of what God was doing through our church, and this prayer has been repeated many times.

We still get tears in our eyes when we see the people God has brought, gathered from so many different backgrounds in order to worship the same God. It is so great to see the church filled again with children learning about Jesus and what he has done for us. If you told us what our church would look like today, we would never have believed you, but God can work miracles.

- Dave & Nancy

DISCUSSION QUESTIONS

1. Consider Luke 14:27-33 again. What does it look like to count the cost of replanting your church?

2. What are some ways in which your church's culture would need to change?

3. Identify some sacred cows in your church.

4. How do you view the community around your church? Does your heart break for it?

5. Which advantages to church replanting appeal to you the most?

6. How can your church building and resources be used for God's glory?

7. What gifts might older saints offer to a replant?

8. What strengths from your church's history might the replant build upon?

Chapter 5

IS OUR CHURCH READY TO BE REPLANTED?

Change. Do you love it or hate it? A 20th-century journalist named Sydney J. Harris once said, "Our dilemma is that we hate change and love it at the same time; what we really want is for things to remain the same but get better." Change is part of life, and whether we like it or not, change is inevitable. It is inevitable in our personal lives, families, communities, world, and even our churches. Being leaders in the church, we must deal with and lead change constantly. Our attitude toward change can positively or negatively affect the rest of the congregation.

As a leader in your church, you are an agent of change, mainly because a leader's job is to help take people and churches from where they are to where they need to be. Of course, this is much easier said than done. In fact, leading change well is one of, if not the most challenging, aspects of serving and leading in a local church context.

Leading change well is a particular challenge when it comes to church replanting. It is difficult for a myriad of reasons, but it is particularly challenging because many dying churches, while understanding real change is needed, are unwilling to do the things that need to be done to become healthy and grow again. Sadly, there are often individuals in these churches who are adamantly opposed to changes of almost any kind. This is one of the reasons why the church is in the condition in which it finds itself.

As you think about your own congregation and the different leaders, families, and personalities that make it up, it is critical to discern whether or not your church is ready for the kind of change that comes with being replanted. I will be the first to say that replanting is not the best option for every declining church. I say this primarily because **a declining church has to want to change if the replant is going to work**. A congregation has to desire to follow through on whatever changes are needed to become a vibrant, growing congregation once again. This chapter is focused on helping you honestly ask and answer strategic questions to help you evaluate your congregation's readiness to change and move forward as a replant.

IS OUR CHURCH READY TO BE REPLANTED?

How do you determine whether or not your church is actually ready to be replanted? Many churches recognize they are struggling and in need of help, but how does one distinguish between a church that is ready to go "all in" as a replant, and a church that is not ready for that step? Specifically, you must measure your church's readiness particularly as it pertains to the giving up of control and decision making. This is where doing honest, strategic assessment and evaluation of your church is absolutely vital.

I've heard it said that the number one job of a leader is to always name reality. What you must do when you're assessing your church's readiness for replanting is to identify where the church really is now. What are the real strengths? What are the real challenges? What are the potential pitfalls? What does your church need to become healthy again? These are the types of questions that must be wrestled with in order to clearly see the reality of the situation.

Before we consider some important questions to ask and answer when assessing your church's readiness for replanting, let me offer four keys to doing this well:

Key #1: Having a Humble and Gracious Heart

You want to pray as you are assessing your church that God will give you a humble heart. You want to pray that God would help you see your congregation with his eyes—full of compassion, love, and grace. "Lord, help me to see our people as You see them. Help me to see our church as You see our church."

Key #2: Being Willing to Honestly Evaluate

When assessing your church, you must be honest about the good, the bad, and the ugly. You must be a realist—a hopeful and faith-filled realist, yes, but a realist all the same. There may be a temptation to unwisely gloss over real issues and challenges that are present in your congregation under the guise of, "God's got this! He'll take care of the tough stuff in this church." While of course God is sovereign and in control of all things and he cares for your congregation deeply, this must never be an excuse for failing to do one's due diligence in assessing the readiness of a congregation for the type of radical change that replanting brings.

Key #3: Having a Hopeful Vision of What Can Be

This is one of the most exciting aspects of replanting: to dream about all that God can do in and through your church! Leading with contagious, joyful, hope-filled vision is crucial in effectively leading your church toward becoming a replant. It can be so easy to feel overwhelmed and discouraged when looking at the things that need to be fixed or changed in a church, but visionary leaders don't let this weigh them down or steal their joy in what God can do. It is vital to dream as you look at your church. What could be? What could the Lord do in and through our congregation? In this community? In the world?

When we lead with hopeful vision, we are leading with eyes of faith. The folks in your congregation desperately need that type of leadership. This kind of hopeful leadership is not focused on what some new program, evangelism strategy, or even pastor can do to revitalize this church, but rather on what God can do in and through your church for his glory. And so you must dream as you're assessing your church, with real faith, hope, and trust.

Key #4: Pursuing Prayerful Wisdom Continually

Through this whole process of assessment, you want to be in heavy prayer—and often! You want to be humble and honest.

You want to have vision. But, most importantly, you want to be constantly praying for God to give you discernment and wisdom from above, not from the world. This is why having several people involved in this assessment process is so important. Different personalities, giftings, and ages are crucial in helping to best discern God's leading in this process. This is not a "one-man" show. It is a community effort. Therefore, you must work together with others from your church to discern and assess the readiness of your congregation for replanting.

THREE GROUPS OF PEOPLE TO HELP YOU DETERMINE YOUR CHURCH'S READINESS FOR REPLANTING

Let's briefly consider three specific groups of people within your church. You will want to talk with each of these groups in order to help determine readiness for replanting. Let me also offer some of the key questions you will want to ask and discuss with each of these groups. Be sure to take notes as you listen to their responses.

Group #1: Older Members and Older Attenders

You're going to want to ask your older members a lot of questions. These are folks who have been part of your church for a long time and who have given much of themselves to your church. It's very likely that they're invested and highly committed even though they may be tired and a bit discouraged. Here are some of the questions to discuss together.

10 Key Questions to Discuss

1. In your opinion, what are the three best things about our church?

2. What do you think the average person in the church would say is the best thing about our church?

3. What is your dream for how our church might look ten years from now?

4. How would you sum up the spiritual health of our congregation in regards to prayer, a heart for evangelism, love for one another, etc.?

5. In your opinion, what are the three biggest challenges in our church right now?

6. What are some of the "sacred cows" (ideas, customs, or traditions that are almost immune—often unreasonably so—from questioning in a church) we need to be aware of?

7. From your perspective as one who has been around for many years, how well does our congregation do with change?

8. Can you share some of the changes that have been made (big or small) in this congregation in the past? How has that been received? Why?

9. How well do you feel our church handles conflict? Can you share an example of a conflict and how it was handled in the past few years?

10. What are a few potentially divisive issues our church could face (practical, doctrinal, personal) moving into the future? Why do you feel this way?

Group #2: Newer Members and Newer Attenders

While there may not be many of these individuals in your church who have been attending for just the past one to two years or less, you want to get to know why they are there. What do they love about your church? What would they like to see happen in the church in the future? Even if it's one young couple or single adult, you want to pick their brains and get their insight. Here are some questions to ask these newer members and attenders:

8 Key Questions to Discuss

1. How did you find out about our church? What caused you to come check us out?

2. In your opinion, what are the three best things about our church?

3. What do you think the average person in the church would say is the best thing about our church?

4. What is your dream for how our church might look 10 years from now?

5. How would you sum up the spiritual health of our congregation in regards to prayer, a heart for evangelism, love for one another, etc.?

6. In your opinion, what are the three biggest challenges in the church right now?

7. As someone who is newer to our church, have you perceived there to be any "sacred cows" others in the church may not be aware of? What are some of those?

8. From your perspective, how well do you feel our congregation does with change? Why do you think that is?

Group #3: Current Leaders of the Church

I'm assuming if you are reading this book that YOU are one of these leaders. Leaders like yourself are probably the most critical group of folks in the church with whom to talk. The leaders in your congregation are most likely the primary influencers in your church. The reason for this is that often when a church is in decline, those with the most influence in the church body step up, out of necessity if nothing else, because someone must lead. You're going to want to intentionally pursue these individuals, asking a lot of questions and doing even more listening. These are the main players who will help make the transition to a replant either a healthy one or a difficult one for your church, should you choose to move in that direction.

Along with discussing with these leaders some of the same questions asked above of older and newer members, the following are additional questions for this specific group. These are tough questions. These are questions that take brutal honesty and humility on the part of your leaders. However, I think these may be the most important questions you can ask at this point in the process. In asking them, you may even determine that you aren't ready yet for replanting. But, remember, the #1 job of a leader is to name reality.

For this reason, I will split these questions into two categories—questions which examine your church's current health (or lack thereof) and questions which examine how far you are willing to go to get better. After all, it is one thing to take your temperature. It's another thing entirely to evaluate the treatment... which in this case is the strategy of replanting.

Part 1: Taking the Temperature
12 Key Questions to Discuss

1. Has our church seen active attendance decline for more than 3 years?

2. Is our church struggling to pay our bills in a timely manner? Has our church been unable to pay our pastor in the manner in which we think he should be paid?

3. Are we struggling to attract young people and young families from our neighborhood/community?

4. If our current trends continue in both attendance and giving, do we fear our church will have to close within the next couple of years?

5. What is our current reputation in the community? Would the community notice, or be affected, if our church closed its doors?

6. Does our church look like the neighborhood which surrounds it (e.g. ethnically, socioeconomically, racially, age, etc.)? If not, why do you think that is the case?

7. What influences have driven our decision-making most? What preferences have held the reigns?

8. What "unofficial" expectations have we had for our pastor? How he uses his time? How he dresses? His preaching capacity? What role his wife has in the church?

9. What idols are fighting most against the life God wants for our church? How do desires for control, comfort, power, or approval fight to rule our church today?

10. What if left unchecked could kill our church?

11. Can our church face the leadership challenge required to turn things around? Or, has our church been on a downward trajectory for so long we have lost the critical mass needed to survive?

12. What makes more sense for our church in this next season of our life together: Pursuing intentional revitalization or intentional replanting?

Part 2: Evaluating the Treatment
10 Key Questions to Discuss

1. Is there a "golden era" of our church we are determined to get back to? How are we tempted to live in the past? Are we content if things never look as they once did?

2. Are we looking for a "magic bullet" to fix things (i.e. a new worship style, pastor, building remodel, outreach strategy, program, etc.)? Do we expect health to come in 2-3 years' time? Or are we willing for it to take 5-10 years?

3. Who or what gets the most blame for the church's current condition (e.g. denomination, immoral culture, previous pastor, young people, lacking/deteriorating facilities, your changing community, etc.)? Are we willing and able to clearly own our contribution?

4. How much influence do bullies and critics have upon the church? How have they been addressed or ignored? Are we willing to address them today?

5. Are any items in the current worship service or building off-limits from change (outside of clear biblical expectations like prayer, preaching, worship, communion, baptism, etc.)? Why?

6. Would this congregation have any objection to the pastor spending a majority of his time outside the church walls, building relationships in the community?

7. Would present ministry leaders be willing to step down if that is what is best for the church moving forward? Why or why not?

8. What financial cuts (including programs, events, or staff positions) are we willing to make in order to care for our new pastor and engage our neighbors who don't know Jesus? What would be the most difficult ones to make?

9. How much have we prayed together about our current state as well as for humility and courage in whatever is to come?

10. How well does the congregation understand what replanting would ask of them? What costs might be most unclear or catch the congregation by surprise? What joys or advantages might they overlook?

THE BOTTOM LINE

The bottom line in all of this is that you want to take seriously the step of evaluating and assessing your church's readiness to be replanted. Perhaps replanting is not the best way to go at this point. Maybe pursuing intentional revitalization is a better step moving forward for your congregation. It is only through honest assessment and evaluation that you will be able to discern what is best for your church. Ask the Lord to give you much humility, wisdom, and courage in all of this. This is his church. He loves your church, and he wants to see it healthy and growing again for your joy, for the good of the community, and for his ultimate glory!

GOD WASN'T DONE WITH OUR CHURCH

Jeff and I (Tyann) met at Southwest Baptist University in Missouri and after finishing college moved back to Denver where we started attending our church. It was the same church I grew up in, where my parents met, and grandparents, and siblings all attended, so it was an easy fit. This church has been a part of our DNA for as long as we can remember. As a young child, I walked down the aisle here, giving my life to Christ. In fact, Jeff, our boys, and I have all been baptized here. This is where we were discipled, where we learned the value of missions and giving, and where we saw the importance of serving in our church. When we walk through the halls, every nook and cranny holds a memory. The church building, people past and present are all a part of our family.

And in my 40 years here, I (Tyann) have seen many highs and lows, not only numerically but also spiritually as well. There have been many godly men and women who poured into us and led us by example, demonstrating lives of prayer and worship. Moreover, it was always fun to be at our church!

But there were tough days too, hard times where we learned humility and our dependence on God. For over time, our church declined, nurturing the members we had but losing touch with our neighbors and community. Instead of raising up new leaders, the same people took on more and more responsibility. We were trying to honor those that had faithfully served for years before us, but this put our focus on tradition rather than on winning souls for Christ. Faced with just a few families, we knew radical change was needed. We needed to open our hands to give control to God. After all, this is his church and his plans to follow.

A short time after, a new pastor came, and he sat down with us to ask where we were serving in the church. We had our hands in everything: women and children's ministries, maintenance, secretarial, and more. Then, he asked us where we *wanted* to serve, not where we felt we *had* to serve. This simple question was life-giving. In fact, it was a turning point for us. It gave us hope and put us in a place where we could take a breath, heal, and serve where we were called to serve.

Looking back over the last 8 years, we have found where we were called to serve—using what we went through to help other churches who are feeling frustrated, desperate, and hopeless. And, it is so rewarding!

If there had been a formal replanting process to follow at the time we would have jumped on it! But our church's revitalization wasn't formal, it was just what came natural as we learned to be in God's Word and allowing him to soften our hearts to change. When you stick in one place for long enough, you get to see a beautiful story of God's faithfulness. There are stories of highs and lows, forgiveness and reconciliation, of promises kept and promises to come. It is a gift not only to share our history with our children, but to know they are being raised in a church that values Scripture and community. Being a part of our church's story has been a blessing beyond measure.

- Jeff & Tyann

DISCUSSION QUESTIONS

1. How could change be introduced in a helpful manner in your church?

2. Do you believe your church is ready to be replanted? Why or why not?

3. What is your dream for what the Lord could do in and through your church?

4. Make a list of people to whom you will ask the suggested questions listed in this chapter.

5. Take time to pray right now for your church, especially for continued grace and humility and for God's wisdom and discernment.

Chapter 6

WHAT ROLE CAN I PLAY?

I can remember sitting down with the core leaders of a dying church that had just voted to be replanted as a new congregation. This was a church that had a rich history of faithfully preaching the gospel and loving their community with the love of Jesus. Sadly, over the years, they struggled to effectively reach the changing neighborhood that surrounded it. While facing what appeared to be imminent death, this congregation eagerly and gladly chose the pathway of replanting.

Our church was privileged to come alongside this congregation and serve them as their sending church. It was a joy to send several faithful families, along with a new pastor that we had been training up to go serve and lead a declining congregation just like this one. By God's grace, this church is now growing once again and is effectively reaching their community with the gospel of Jesus Christ. But what I remember most about the day this church voted to become a replant is the humble posture of their leaders in that room. I can remember their genuine desire to do all that they needed to do to help make this replant a success. A willingness to lay down their preferences for the sake of others that their church might experience new life and vitality.

If you share this same heart, you need to know how honoring this is to the Lord. This kind of selfless, Christ-like, Kingdom-minded attitude is so glorifying to God! This is the kind of attitude that lies at the heart of every legacy congregation I know of that has been successfully replanted.

What Is a "Legacy" Congregation?

The legacy congregation is made up of the remaining folks in the dying congregation that will potentially be replanted. We use the term legacy to communicate our affirmation and desire to celebrate and build off of the God-honoring legacy of this congregation in the new replant. The men and women who are in your church *right now* comprise this legacy congregation!

If you chose to pursue the strategy of replanting, I want to offer two primary practices that you as the legacy congregation can implement to actively support the replant, and joyfully play the role to which God has called you.

PRACTICE #1: SUPPORT YOUR NEW REPLANTING PASTOR AND HIS FAMILY HOWEVER YOU CAN.

Replanting is not for everyone. It takes a particular gift mix and a clear calling from the Lord. And, like every other ministry, serving as a pastor of a church replant can be at times very discouraging. There are ups and downs when replanting a congregation. Consider a few of the unique challenges a replanter faces.

It is discouraging when young families come and visit but don't stay because you can't offer the same types of children's programming that the large church down the street does. It is lonely at times as a replanter. Loneliness is one of the leading factors for why a large number of pastors quit ministry altogether. The legacy congregation must help him fight against this feeling of loneliness that is so common in ministry. It is tough as a leader when it seems like the congregation is not catching your vision for living on mission and reaching the lost in the community.

It is really hard work to replant a church. No pastor can do this on his own. He needs help. One of the primary sources of help and support should be the legacy congregation. Your congregation will need to help lighten the load so that this replanting work is a joy and not a burden for the replanter, his family, and the newly replanted congregation. It is tiring on a replanter when it feels like even the smallest change he tries to implement is met with pushback.

For these reasons, and many others, it is vital that the leaders of the legacy congregation intentionally work to encourage, assist, and cooperate with the replanter and his family with grace and care over the long haul. (This will most likely require the laying down of some personal preferences for the good of the body.) This is honoring to the Lord, comforting and refreshing for the replanter, and is necessary for the congregation's long-term health and growth.

So, what exactly should this look like practically? Let's consider several ways your congregation can come alongside to care for the replanter and the replanter's family.

Encourage, encourage, encourage!

In 1 Thessalonians 5:11, the Apostle Paul writes to the believers in Thessalonica, "Therefore encourage one another and build one another up, just as you are doing." Paul knew the power of encouragement. He knew that in a fallen and broken world, encouragement is needed more than ever. Sadly, it is rare.

Life is hard. Ministry is hard. Replanting is hard. Replanters often feel discouraged and are not surrounded by many, if any, encouragers. They often hear more words of criticism and complaint than words of praise and thanks. They have to learn a new church culture, they have likely left all of their friends, and they are working long hours for little pay. Add to this the fact that we are all fighting against an enemy that seeks to kill and destroy the work of God. Replanting is a battle. You as part of the legacy congregation can be on the front lines by being a strong source of encouragement for the replanter: Send him notes of thanks; share with him stories of how God is moving in your church; speak words of loving encouragement regarding his preaching; let him know how you personally are growing in Christ; walk with him in a helpful and supportive manner over the course of months and years. He will need it!

While it is critical for your congregation to intentionally encourage and care for the replanter, it is just as important that you care for and encourage the replanter's wife and children. Ministry of any kind can be very hard on a pastor's family. Replanting a church brings unique pressures and challenges that not only affect the replanter, but also affect his wife and kids. It is loving, kind, and God-glorifying to prioritize showing extra care and encouragement to the replanter's family. Get creative and have fun showing them the love of Jesus!

Joyfully follow his leadership.

One of the greatest challenges in pastoral ministry is trying to lead a congregation that has a number of critics, naysayers, and contrarians. Instead of following their pastor with humility and joy, these individuals stubbornly rebel against his leadership on a regular basis. This should not be—not for a true man or woman of God who loves the Body of Christ. The writer of Hebrews reminds us, "Obey your leaders and submit to them, for they are keeping watch over your souls, as those who will have to give an account. Let them do this with joy and not with groaning, for that would be of no advantage to you" (Heb. 13:17).

The role we have as members of a congregation is to willingly and gladly support and submit to the leadership of our pastors. The Word of God is clear on this. When we seek to cause our pastor anxiety or harm (even if we think we have the good of the Body in mind), we are in clear opposition to God and his will for the church. As Shawn Wilhite, assistant professor of Christian studies at California Baptist University, writes, "A direct correlation exists between your obedience and [your pastor's] joy. Work hard to submit—gladly, not begrudgingly—to their leadership. It's your Savior's means of providing spiritual oversight to your soul."[1]

If your congregation chooses to replant, one of the best things you can do for your pastor is to joyfully follow his leadership. This is the man God has given to lead and shepherd your congregation. He is there to love you, feed you, protect you, and care for your soul. Honor him, respect him, and follow him with joy. This is good and pleasing to the Lord!

Pray for and with him.

Replanting pastors need prayer. They need lots and lots of prayer! The reality is that they face very unique temptations and pressures every day. Satan hates what God is doing through a pastor's life and ministry and will daily look for new ways to attack and deceive him. For these reasons and so many more, you must pray for him. Pray for him, and pray with him. Consider these 8 ways you can intentionally pray for your replanting pastor and his family.[2]

8 Prayers for Your Replanting Pastor

#1. Protection from Satan

Be sober-minded; be watchful. Your adversary the devil prowls around like a roaring lion, seeking someone to devour.

- 1 Peter 5:8

#2. Protection Against His Own Sinful Heart

But each person is tempted when he is lured and enticed by his own desire. Then desire when it has conceived gives birth to sin, and sin when it is fully grown brings forth death.

- James 1:14-15

#3. Deep Spiritual Encouragement

For I long to see you, that I may impart to you some spiritual gift to strengthen you— that is, that we may be mutually encouraged by each other's faith, both yours and mine.

- Romans 1:11-12

#4. Wisdom

If any of you lacks wisdom, let him ask God, who gives generously to all without reproach, and it will be given him.

- James 1:5

#5. Doctrinal Faithfulness

By the Holy Spirit who dwells within us, guard the good deposit entrusted to you.

- 2 Timothy 1:14

#6. Healthy Body

But I discipline my body and keep it under control, lest after preaching to others I myself should be disqualified.

- 1 Corinthians 9:27

#7. A Strong Marriage and Family

Therefore, an overseer must be above reproach, the husband of one wife, sober-minded, self-controlled, respectable, hospitable, able to teach, not a drunkard, not violent but gentle, not quarrelsome, not a lover of money. He must manage his own household well, with all dignity keeping his children submissive, for if someone does not know how to manage his own household, how will he care for God's church?

- 1 Timothy 3:2-6

#8. Meaningful Friendships

A man of many companions may come to ruin, but there is a friend who sticks closer than a brother.

- Proverbs 18:24

Your prayers will be a source of great strength and encouragement to your pastor as he seeks to lead this new replant. As James writes in the last part of James 5:16, "The prayer of a righteous person has great power as it is working." May you gladly pray for your pastor and his family!

Allow him guiltless vacation and rest time.

Make sure the replanter and his family are able to take generous amounts of vacation and rest time. Help them to feel good and not guilty about it. This is not only healthy for their family, it is healthy for the long-term growth and maturity of the replant.

Pastor Ben Haley writes with great wisdom:

Intentional rest is absolutely critical to the long term health of pastors, bringing rejuvenation and renewal to the rhythm of pastoral ministry. This kind of rest and readjustment is important because it is important to God! We live in a face-paced, distraction-filled world. The demands of families, friends, jobs, church life, volunteering, and the like will always ask more of us than we have the capacity to give...which teaches us all dependence on Christ and His strength, the empowering of His Spirit, and a regular rhythm of resting in Him. In this rest, we are reminded of our identity in Him, our sinful motives are exposed, and we can breathe deeply of the gospel and finished work of Jesus on our behalf. This is the kind of soulful rest that then becomes the gasoline in the engine of our hard work. It is a critical rhythm not only for pastors...but for all of us![3]

Replanting pastors often have a difficult time leaving their congregation without feeling guilty. Please do all you can to counter this! Help out by offering to step in to help cover the bases while the pastor is on vacation.

PRACTICE #2: SUPPORT YOUR NEW REPLANTED CONGREGATION HOWEVER YOU CAN.

Along with supporting your replanter and his family, a second practice that will greatly help this new replant succeed is for members of the legacy congregation to be huge cheerleaders, active participants, and committed teammates in the life and mission of this new church. For this replant to be all that God wants it to be and all the community needs it to be, it will take church leaders and members who love God, love one another, love the lost, and desire to do whatever it takes to see this new church thrive! In my experience, it takes five biblical, God-honoring commitments on the part of your congregation.

Commitment #1: To Pursue Humility before God and Others

When we look at Scripture, it is clear that the Lord desires humility in his people—humility before God and others. When it comes to playing a supportive role in a new replant, the Lord is looking for men and women who are humble. Those who are humble are the ones he most desires to use for his purposes and his glory.

The Scriptures talk about humility all over the place. Let's look at a few examples. In James 4:6 we read, "God opposes the proud, but gives grace to the humble." James is clear that God is drawn to humble hearts. He opposes an arrogant and prideful heart. He loves to use those with a soft, teachable, humble heart.

In Luke 14:11, Jesus says this, "For everyone who exalts himself will be humbled, and he who humbles himself will be exalted." Again we see that God has no problem humbling those who exalt themselves—humbling those who put themselves above others and who are more concerned with meeting their own needs and desires than helping to meet the needs and desires of others. What this replant needs is men and women who have humble hearts that care more about others than themselves—men and women who are willing to do whatever it takes, putting their own preferences aside, in order to see lives changed and Jesus made famous in their community.

Commitment #2: To Love God and Love People—All Different Kinds of People

What is the most important thing to God? This is a good question. While we could come up with a whole list of different guesses, there is one right answer. Jesus gives us the answer in Mark chapter 12. In this passage a scribe comes up to Jesus and asks him this very question. Starting in verse 28 we read:

> And one of the scribes came up...and asked him, "Which commandment is the most important of all?" Jesus answered, "The most important is, 'Hear, O Israel: The Lord our God, the

Lord is one. And you shall love the Lord your God with all your heart and with all your soul and with all your mind and with all your strength.' The second is this: 'You shall love your neighbor as yourself.' There is no other commandment greater than these.

When you and I die, hopefully there will be a lot of nice things that are said about us at our funerals. There will probably be funny stories told and sweet memories shared. But if, at our funerals, the two things that are not spoken of most are our love for God and our love for people, then according to Jesus, we've missed it. We've missed the mark. We've missed the whole point of this life.

I don't know about you, but if Jesus says this is the most important thing, then I better believe it is the most important thing. Our lives must be marked by love above all else. In replanting, love for God and others must be the primary mark of our lives as members and leaders of this new church.

- **Love for the Lord** that leads to joyful obedience to his Word.
- **Love for the church** that leads to surrendering personal preferences for the sake of others and their needs.
- **Love for the lost** that leads to a courageous, Spirit-filled commitment to do whatever it takes to reach them with the gospel.

Love is the fruit of a genuinely saved person—a person who is now united to Jesus Christ in faith, through his finished work on the cross. What the Lord has called you to is love. What this replant will need from you is love.

Commitment #3: To Speak Words that Bring Life (not Death) to Others

Words are powerful. They can be life-giving and life-changing, or they can be life-damaging and life-destroying. This new replant needs folks who will speak words that bring life and not death to others in the congregation. Look at these verses, specifically the graphic nature of the descriptions used, from the book of Proverbs:

> Death and life are in the power of the tongue. — Proverbs 18:21
> Anxiety in a man's heart weighs him down, but a good word makes him glad. — Proverbs 12:25
>
> The tongue that brings healing is a tree of life, but a deceitful tongue crushes the spirit. — Proverbs 15:4
>
> Gracious words are like a honeycomb, sweetness to the soul and health to the body. — Proverbs 16:24
>
> Let no corrupting talk come out of your mouths, but only such as is good for building up, as fits the occasion, that it may give grace to those who hear. — Ephesians 4:29

One of the greatest ways you can support this new replant is through committing to speak words that bring life and not death to others. Instead of words of grumbling, saturate others in this congregation with words that build up. What a joy it is to use our words in this helpful, life-giving, God-honoring manner! Words like this are a catalyst for great joy in your church.

Commitment #4: To Live and Minister in Unity

Replanting a church is a very exciting journey. To see the Lord begin to bring a declining church back to health and vibrancy is an amazing thing to witness and be a part of. And yet, it is often when God is doing incredible things in a new replant that Satan seeks to bring disunity, dissension, and division in that church body. It is also in times when God is doing the most amazing things that our sinful nature can rear its ugly head. Instead of rejoicing and praising God for his work, serving the church with delight, and encouraging other brothers and sisters in the congregation, we can become self-absorbed, bitter, and prideful. All of this can bring about a deadly spirit of disunity to a new replant.

One of the greatest gifts you can bring to this new church is a spirit of unity. In 1 Corinthians 1:10, Paul urges the believers in Corinth, along with us, to pursue unity when he writes, "I appeal to you, brothers, by the name of our Lord Jesus Christ, that all of you agree, and that there be no divisions among you, but that you be united in the same mind and the same judgment."

While Satan seeks to bring division, may you be one who pursues peace and unity with others. May you join our Savior when He prays to the Father for our unity as his followers in John 17:21, that we as believers might "all be one, just as you, Father, are in me, and I in you, that they also may be in us, so that the world may believe that you have sent me." As we seek to be pursuers of unity rather than disunity, Jesus says the lost will take notice, and the Lord will use this loving witness to draw them to himself! What an amazing promise. In this new replant, ask God to help you live and minister in unity, for the sake of the lost and for the delight of God.

Commitment #5: To Pray

Prayer must be a top priority in your church replanting efforts. We can do nothing apart from the mercy and power of God. In prayer we are calling out to him, admitting our need, and trusting in his sovereign grace. Let me encourage you to make a joyful commitment to pray for this new congregation.

So, what should you pray? How should you pray? I'll list several specific ways you can pray for this replant. It would likely also be worthwhile to brainstorm creative ways you can equip and encourage others in the legacy congregation to pray for these things on a regular and consistent basis. For older members who have a difficult time getting around and attending various events and activities, this is a great way to help them feel connected to what is happening as they pray for specific needs of the replant.

12 Prayers for the Replant

1. Pray the replant and its leaders will keep their eyes on God and not take a step apart from God's leading.

2. Pray for courage and boldness to go where the Lord leads.

3. Pray for humility before the Lord and people, prioritizing the raising up of other leaders.

4. Pray the replant and its leaders will not rely on their own strength, but trust in the Lord's strength.

5. Pray for a deep heart of love for those leading this new replant.

6. Pray for the health of marriages and families in the congregation.

7. Pray the replant and its leaders will walk worthy of the calling God has placed on their lives.

8. Pray for the replanter to preach the Word and the gospel boldly.

9. Pray for God to destroy idols in the hearts of the leaders and in the hearts of those in the congregation.

10. Pray for God-honoring unity in the congregation.

11. Pray the replant and its leaders will do whatever it takes to reach the lost.

12. Pray for the making of disciples who make disciples in and through the replant.

IT'S ALL ABOUT THE LONG HAUL...

If you choose to pursue replanting your congregation, it is a wonderful, challenging, exciting journey of faith! As the legacy congregation, the replanter and the new church will need your steady love, support, encouragement, and prayer. The replanter's wife and kids will also need your faithful care, not just for a few days or weeks, but for months and even years into the future. May the Lord, by his grace and power, give you all that you need to love these dear brothers and sisters in Christ with the intentional, radical, selfless, love of Jesus over the long haul.

GOD **WASN'T** DONE WITH OUR CHURCH

My church (Krysti) has always meant love and family to me and was a place to call "home." I grew up in the children's and youth ministries at my church and loved it there. There I learned how to read my Bible, to memorize Scripture and to serve. But most importantly, I learned how to love Jesus and to love others.

In the early 2000's, our church went through a lot of change. We had a pastor retire and went through a few interim pastors. Attendance had declined significantly, and there were a handful of people (mostly members of my family and extended family) working hard to keep the doors open. I was in my college years and was attending different church programs in the area for people my age. But the church was still "home" to me, and all of my family was still there.

In 2006, Richard and I got married, and since he worked on Sundays, I started attending the church full-time again. By then attendance had picked back up, but finances were still very tight. And, it seemed like it was still the small handful of people doing most of the work, serving in areas of necessity. It was difficult to find the joy in this work, and it felt as though spiritual growth had become an afterthought.

For years, my dad and I would talk about how we felt that God was not done with our church yet, so we all just kept on. But, it was exhausting and lonely. So when the opportunity to revitalize came along in 2009, the core group jumped at the opportunity. We felt that God had big plans for our church, but we knew that we were tired and needed help.

When we finally started to grow in numbers and the core group got some help, it felt like the fruits of our labor started to show. Spiritual growth had become the priority again, and we were able to serve out of the overflow in areas where we were passionate. I served in the youth ministry and got to pour life into teenage girls with a team of people who had the same vision and passion.

The growth also brought some younger married couples and families who were in the same life stage as Richard and I, and we enjoyed doing life with them. We also had a friend come back to the Lord in late 2009, and because our church had life, he was able to continue his growth. We had our son, Brent, at the end of 2010, and he was one of eight or nine children born into our church family within a year and a half of the revitalization. We were all (mostly) new moms and dads at the time, and together we learned what it means to be godly parents.

Then in 2013, Richard, Brent and I joined the core team for our church's first church plant. It was a bittersweet decision, since we loved our community at the church as well as attending and serving with my family. But ultimately, we felt it was where God wanted us, and we love it. We both serve where we feel called, and all three of us have made some dear friends here. Since then, we have watched our churches plant, replant, and revitalize so many more churches that I cannot keep track!

We have grown in so many ways and have had many blessings since the revitalization we experienced in 2009, but the biggest blessing came earlier this year when my dad, Doug, passed away. My dad loved our church, and he was one of the handful of people working hard to keep the doors open during the hard times. He loved to see the Lord working through the growing network of churches. And in his final hours, we had no shortage of people coming to pay their respects to my dad, sharing stories about how he had impacted their lives.

We had at least six churches in this network represented at the hospital... and had our church not gone through the revitalization process years ago, we would not have had that support. We will forever be grateful for the love, encouragement, growth and help we have received as result!

- Richard & Krysti

DISCUSSION QUESTIONS

1. In what ways can a church replanter's job be difficult?

2. How can you show support and encouragement to your new pastor?

3. How can you show love and care to your pastor's family?

4. How can you help and encourage the rest of the congregation?

5. Stop and pray right now for your new pastor, his family, and your congregation. Ask the Lord to shower his grace, mercy, wisdom, joy, and perseverance on each one of you.

Chapter 7

WHAT'S NEXT?

God's not done with your church!

That is the primary message of this book, and I pray it brings encouragement and hope to you and to others in your congregation. We serve an awesome and mighty God who does his greatest work when things seem most bleak, when things feel hopeless. This is true in our individual lives, and it is true in our churches. *His strength is perfect when our strength is gone!*

Hear some of these hope-filled truths from God's Word. May they encourage you as you read them:

> But he said to me, "My grace is sufficient for you, for my power is made perfect in weakness." Therefore I will boast all the more gladly of my weaknesses, so that the power of Christ may rest upon me. – 2 Corinthians 12:9

> Have you not known? Have you not heard? The Lord is the everlasting God, the Creator of the ends of the earth. He does not faint or grow weary; his understanding is unsearchable. He gives power to the faint, and to him who has no might he increases strength. Even youths shall faint and be weary, and young men

shall fall exhausted; but they who wait for the Lord shall renew their strength; they shall mount up with wings like eagles; they shall run and not be weary; they shall walk and not faint. – Isaiah 40:28-31

Let us then with confidence draw near to the throne of grace, that we may receive mercy and find grace to help in time of need. – Hebrews 4:16

May the God of hope fill you with all joy and peace in believing, so that by the power of the Holy Spirit you may abound in hope. – Romans 15:13

I have said these things to you, that in me you may have peace. In the world you will have tribulation. But take heart; I have overcome the world." - John 16:33

Take my yoke upon you, and learn from me, for I am gentle and lowly in heart, and you will find rest for your souls. – Matthew 11:29

Fear not, for I am with you; be not dismayed, for I am your God; I will strengthen you, I will help you, I will uphold you with my righteous right hand. – Isaiah 41:10

Finally, be strong in the Lord and in the strength of his might. – Ephesians 6:10

We could spend hours reading verse after verse in Scripture that echoes the very same truth: *The Lord is our Rock and he is a God who loves to bring hope to the hopeless, sight to the blind, strength to the weary.* He is the God who brings beauty out of that which appears to have none. He is the God who redeems and restores broken things, who shines light into the darkness, who brings dead bones back to life. He is the God who loves to do all of these things in and through struggling churches just like yours.

I know how painful and devastating it can be to see the church you love slipping away rather than growing in health and vibrancy. The pain of wondering, "Is this the end?" It doesn't have to be! As I pray you have seen throughout this book, there is real hope and real help for churches just like yours. In light of all that we have considered in the previous chapters, I want to leave you with some very simple, concrete steps to help you apply some of what you have read in these pages.

FIVE NEXT STEPS

Step #1: Seek God's leading through prayer and Scripture.

Too many struggling churches begin their search for help and assistance by looking anywhere and everywhere other than God himself. Yes, it is wise to pursue godly counsel from other churches, pastors, and denominational leaders, but I would encourage you to seek God's face first. Ultimately, this is his church. He cares more about the revitalization and health of your congregation than you do! Plus, let's be honest, he alone has the power to do the things that need to be done in revitalizing your congregation. He is the living God!

The place to begin then is on your knees in prayer. As we see all throughout the Scriptures, the Lord uses the prayers of his people in mighty ways. This is what you and your church need more than anything else. You need God to move in power! You need God to do the impossible. And the amazing thing about our God is that he invites us to bring our fears, burdens, requests, and supplications to him. What an amazing promise that we read in 1 John 5:14-15, "And this is the confidence that we have toward him, that if we ask anything according to his will he hears us. And if we know that he hears us in whatever we ask, we know that we have the requests that we have asked of him."

Ultimately, as we bring our hearts to God in prayer, we also come to him in submission to his Word, seeking his truth and his will. The Lord speaks to us through his Word. He brings clarity in the midst of confusion through his Word. He gives to us what James calls, wisdom from above, through his Word. That is, wisdom from God himself. In contrast, wisdom from below is worldly wisdom. The last thing you and your church need at this point in time is worldly wisdom, unfruitful gimmicks and false promises of "quick fixes" that ultimately fix nothing at all. You need the Lord to give you wisdom from above as you seek what is best for your struggling church. As James writes in chapter 3, verse 17, "...wisdom from above is first pure, then peaceable, gentle, open to reason, full of mercy and good fruits, impartial and sincere." This is the kind of wisdom that God wants to give you and that will help you rightly discern what is best for your church and your community moving forward. This is the kind of wisdom that will empower you to walk by faith, trusting the Lord in ways that will bring him much glory.

Step #2: Honestly evaluate your church's current condition.

As mentioned earlier, the number #1 job of a leader is to name reality. This can be incredibly painful, but it is absolutely critical. Sadly, many declining churches do not have leaders that honestly evaluate their church's current condition. For some it takes energy they do not have. For others, it is simply too difficult to acknowledge the unhealthy situation their church is in. I am sympathetic to this. I really am. No one wants to take a deep, hard look at the condition of their struggling church and have to admit they need serious help. It is hard. It is sad. It is difficult. This is why many try to avoid honestly naming their church's sickness at all costs. However, the only way to health and healing is to name the reality of the illness. In the same way that going to the doctor helps no one if we are never given an accurate diagnosis of our sickness, failing to accurately assess the condition of your declining church will make it impossible to find the help and healing you need.

Be sure to look back at Chapter 5 as it will help coach you through this step of honestly evaluating your church's current condition. As you spend time with the different groups of folks mentioned, asking these individuals some of the questions listed for you, among others you come up with, I believe you will gain helpful, much needed insight. Having a good grasp on the thoughts and feelings of those in your congregation will help you prepare for the next step.

Step #3: Pursue counsel and wisdom from outside of your church.

The next step in helping you discern where God is leading your church is to pursue counsel and wisdom from friends and leaders from outside of your church. The Bible is very clear that wisdom comes when we seek godly counsel from others. This is particularly true when we find ourselves at a major crossroads in our life and it isn't clear which way the Lord wants us to go. Perhaps you feel like your church is at that type of crossroads right now. The book of Proverbs is filled with verses that speak to the importance of seeking godly counsel. Consider these:

> The way of a fool is right in his own eyes, but a wise man listens to advice. – Proverbs 12:15

> Where there is no guidance, a people falls, but in an abundance of counselors there is safety. – Proverbs 11:14

> Without counsel plans fail, but with many advisers they succeed. – Proverbs 15:22

You and your church need to pursue this type of godly counsel at this point in time. Wisdom that comes from godly individuals who are not part of your church. These men and women can offer insight and helpful perspective as those who are not as intimately connected to your congregation as you are. They can help you think through tough questions and issues pertaining to your church's future in an unbiased, godly, objective manner. So who exactly are these outside counselors you ought to seek counsel from? Where do you find them? Here are three groups to consider pursuing.

Group #1: Denominational & Network Leaders

Contact your area denominational and network leaders. These leaders exist for the sole purpose of helping churches to be more effective in gospel ministry. Most of these leaders have been trained on some level to come alongside declining and struggling churches like yours to help bring support, encouragement, counsel, and connections to others within your denomination or network who can also be of assistance to you and your church in this time. These leaders can also bring helpful resources to your replanting or revitalization process moving forward.

Goup #2: Seminaries & Bible Schools

Reach out to seminaries and Bible schools in your area. Many times you will find professors at seminaries who have experience pastoring in local church contexts and specialize in helping churches that are dying. It is well worth connecting with your denomination's seminary to see if there is a faculty member you can speak with. Most likely, you will find someone who can offer helpful insight for your situation, as well as connect you to others who can be of help.

Group #3: Local Pastors & Churches

Connect with local pastors and churches in your community. There are many pastors and churches in your community that would love to help your church however they can. At a minimum, you will find pastors and individuals in these churches that would love to come alongside and offer godly wisdom and counsel to you. However, along with counsel, many times there are leaders in churches within your community who would love to see their congregation partner with your congregation, as you seek to become a healthy, vibrant church once again. Unfortunately, while there are always some who feel threatened by other churches in their community, I believe there are many others that care more about the Kingdom of God than just their own church. As Christians, we are all in this together. In fact, we are always at our best when we cooperate with eagerness and joyful humility. This is especially true when it comes to helping our brothers and sisters in Christ who are struggling. Don't be afraid to reach out to pastors and churches in your community. The family of God is there to help you!

Step #4: Bring a recommendation to your congregation.

In most declining churches, the remaining members are very tired and are looking to an individual or small group of individuals like you to guide them and lead them in this discernment process. Once you have spent time seeking the Lord through prayer and the Word, honestly evaluating the current condition of your church, and pursuing counsel and wisdom from those on the outside, it is probably time for you to bring some kind of recommendation to your congregation on how best to move forward. It is worth noting that many times a denominational leader can be of great help in assisting you and your church in putting together and thinking through this kind of recommendation.

The recommendation that you bring to your congregation will probably focus on one of the following options.

Option #1: Close your church.

This option is probably the simplest option for a dying church to choose. This is the option whereby your church ceases to exist as a church and agrees to turn over the building and all assets to your denomination, an outside approved ministry partner, or new church plant. Here's the problem. Mark Clifton is right when he writes,

> Although this one may be the simplest of all approaches in replanting, it can also be the most difficult for the struggling church to accept. It isn't easy for a church that has a long history of ministry in a building to decide to simply hand it over to a new generation.[1]

This is very true. While I understand that in some cases this is the best and perhaps only option for a congregation given their lack of health, this can be an incredibly painful way to go. This is why I wrote this book. To help churches like yours see that this is not the only option. Closing your doors once and for all is not the only option! Remember, God does his best work in our weakness. When things seem hopeless. For this reason, this option, in my opinion, should be the last resort if at all possible.

Option #2: Revitalize your church.

This is the church revitalization option. As discussed earlier, revitalization is the deliberate, dedicated and protracted effort to reverse the decline or death of an existing church like yours. In Chapter 1, we considered several characteristics, both positive and negative, for choosing this option. Let's review a few of these again:

Church Revitalization

- The **least** invasive approach as few major changes are made up front.

- Utilizes **existing** structures, leadership and congregants.

- May be led by an existing or **new pastor**. (Revitalization is less likely to occur successfully with a long tenured existing pastor; more likely, a new pastor will be the best way to move forward).

- Requires a **great deal of time**—the pace of change is very slow.

- **High risk** as the church may reject the leadership efforts of the pastor and leaders and ask them to leave or remove them through elevated conflict or forced termination.

- Is less likely to lead to lasting change and more likely to be a **continuation** of the same.

- Is the **least** effective approach for churches facing imminent closure.

While revitalization may be the best option for your church, and while it may be the easiest for everyone in your congregation to agree to, it is critically important to understand the bullet points above. Revitalization is a very slow process with no guarantee that major change will actually happen in your church. Because there are no major changes to the leadership structure, decision making process, or existing ministry programs, this option can often give the impression that a church is moving toward healthy change without actually changing much of anything at all.

The most obvious risk here is that while in the short term the decision to move toward revitalization may be easiest to approve, ruffling the least amount of feathers, it could make it much more difficult to lead real, lasting change for the long term. If your congregation chooses this option, it must be understood by all that effective revitalization not only takes time, and not only takes great humility and unity on the part of the remaining members, but it also takes strong, committed leadership from both the pastor and lay leaders. Courageous, Christ-like leadership that can lovingly yet firmly lead your congregation outward on mission in your community for the long haul.

Option #3: Replant your church.

This third option, the option to replant your congregation, is what I believe to be the most effective pathway to new life, health and vitality for churches like yours. This replanting pathway is what we have considered most deeply throughout this book.

When a church chooses to be replanted, they choose to re-launch itself as a new church, with new leadership (a new replanting pastor), new name, new identity, new governance, new ministry approach and overall new philosophy of ministry. Just as we did with revitalization, let's review some of the characteristics of replanting:

Church Replanting

- Builds on the **history/legacy** of the previous church.

- Requires **new leadership** (a new replanting pastor).

- New decision-making structure and new decision makers who handle the **daily decisions** (outside transition team).

- New **by-laws** are created and put into practice.

- Offers a break with the past (end date) and a **fresh start** for the future (launch date).

- New **identity** can create excitement, momentum, enthusiasm and interest in the community.

The key to helping your church pursue this replanting option is identifying a strong outside transition team that can help support, guide and direct you. This transition team could be a group made up of pastors and leaders from different churches in your community. It could be a group of denominational or network leaders. It might be a combination of both. Typically, someone from your denomination or network can help assist you in finding and assembling an outside transition team for your church. If you aren't sure who to talk with, or have no connection with a denominational or network leader, feel free to email sendme@namb.net for assistance. Here you will find replanting specialists who can help get you started and pointed in the right direction.

As mentioned earlier, while I recognize it's not always possible, one of the most effective ways to replant a congregation like yours is by joyfully partnering with and surrendering to an outside transition team made up of pastors and leaders from another congregation. A congregation that has a vision to help replant struggling churches. *This congregation is called a sending church.* This is a congregation that would come alongside your church with love and support, linking arms with your congregation for the long haul, helping to lead you through the replanting process. With a sending church, you not only get an outside transition team to help you, *but you get an entire congregation to help you*!

We can't do this alone, which is why I would strongly encourage your church to come under the care and leadership of a sending church, if it is at all possible. If you are wondering where to find a sending church to help you, look to the Appendix where I address the question: *How does our congregation find the right sending church to lead us in this replanting process?*

Step #5: Trust God and move forward in humility and faith.

Once you and your congregation have chosen one of the three options above to pursue, the next step is to simply trust God and move forward in humility and faith. You belong to the Lord. Your church belongs to the Lord. And that is a good thing. He is the all-wise, sovereign and merciful God of the universe and he holds the whole world in his hands. That includes your church. Your job now is to trust him. Trust him with your church. Trust him with humble faith. Faith like a child. Faith that believes what God said to Joshua so many years ago is just as true for us today, "Be strong and courageous. Do not be frightened, and do not be dismayed, for the LORD your God is with you wherever you go (Joshua 1:9)."

You and your church are now entering a new season. Whatever it looks like, the Lord has a good purpose for it. For we know from God's perfect Word in Romans 8:28 that, "…for those who love God all things work together for good, for those who are called according to his purpose." Whatever lies ahead, the Lord is going to use it for good in your life and in the life of your church. For your joy and the joy of your congregation. More than that, whatever now lies ahead God will use to bring himself the glory he so richly deserves!

GOD'S NOT DONE...

The truth is, God loves struggling churches and desires to bring them back to life and vibrancy for the sake of his Name. This includes your church! And the amazing thing is that he invites us to be a part of it. Know that I am cheering for your church, and my prayer is that you would not lose hope or give up! Many once-dying churches are now becoming healthy again, engaging their communities and reaching the lost with the power of Christ in new and exciting ways. It's happening! The Lord is doing this kind of replanting work all over our country and world for his glory and the joy of his Church. I truly believe he wants to do the same in your church! Can you imagine? God is not done with your church!

GOD **ISN'T** DONE
WITH OUR CHURCH

Our replant journey began when our Sr. Pastor announced that he was leaving to accept a position in a church closer to his home in Ohio. During the months preceding pastor's exit, there were many families that left our church for various reasons. And due to this decline in our attendance and less-than-stellar effectiveness at reaching new people, a few of us gathered to discuss what options we had next.

We decided that the best approach was to be intentional in our focus and to dedicate some serious time and attention to the situation. And so, we formed a CCR team (Committee for Church Revitalization) and made this issue a priority in our Wednesday prayer meetings. Spending time on our knees in prayer, we asked God to reveal the approaches other declining/dying churches had taken and what he wanted us to do. After some research, we discovered some books that discussed the challenges and opportunities of church revitalization and the different approaches available.

The next step involved the CCR team deciding to spend several weeks/months reading and discussing the book *Reclaiming Glory* by Mark Clifton and evaluating our situation in light of the others highlighted in his book. This approach helped to facilitate several great discussions in which we determined that our church was quickly reaching a critical decision point: Either we could continue down our current path toward decline only to see our church close its doors like so many others, or with God's guidance and direction, we would make the changes necessary to move off the declining slope and onto a new path of revitalization and renewal, one that would see God glorified as we once again effectively reached lost souls.

The challenge was to find which path would be the most effective and would honor God's will for our church. We weren't sure, but we kept lifting our requests to God.

Here's what God did for us...

One of our members was traveling with his family back to Iowa to visit his parents, and before leaving on this trip, we discussed the opportunity for him to meet with the leadership of his former church (Cornerstone) to discuss our situation. It was a very large and vibrant church with an effective ministry approach, and the intent was to discuss any available options for resources or partnership in our revitalization efforts.

The outcome of the meeting, however, was a bit discouraging, as the leadership indicated that they had no real experience with efforts like this. Discouragement, however, turned quickly to hope, as the very next day, they met someone who did. Soon after our initial meeting, the Cornerstone leadership had dinner with a leader from the Calvary Family of Churches (Jeff) who was attending a seminar in the area devoted to the topic of replanting/revitalization, and Cornerstone immediately connected us.

This meeting catalyzed an amazing journey for our church, and we knew it was no coincidence. This was God's divine appointment, bringing us together at the right place at the right time.

Following this first meeting, we began correspondence with the Calvary Family in order to better understand their approach to church revitalization and how they could help us achieve our goal of making Jesus non-ignorable in Nampa and beyond. And after several phone calls, email exchanges, and video conference calls, our CCR team felt very strongly that God was calling us to replant our church under the sponsorship of the Calvary Family of Churches. God had opened so many doors that pointed us in this direction that we felt confident he was in favor of our moving forward.

Prior to bringing a formal recommendation before the church, we invited Jeff from the Calvary Family to come to Nampa for a weekend workshop to share their approach to church replanting and revitalization with area pastors as well as the members and regular attendees from our church. The atmosphere of these sessions was overwhelmingly positive, and the response from those in attendance was equally inspiring. A lot of interest was generated not only from our church members but other churches in the valley as well. The weekend concluded with Jeff preaching a message on revitalization for the church and a time of question and answer following the service.

Two weeks later, the CCR team brought a formal proposal to join the Calvary Family of Churches through a replant sponsorship, that through them God would breathe new life into our church. Our church voted overwhelmingly and enthusiastically to accept the proposal and begin the next chapter of God's plan for our ministry to reach people in Nampa and beyond with the Good News of Jesus Christ!

Several intentional actions were key in this outcome…

- Realizing that our church was on a current path that would result in eventually closing the doors

- Making an intentional decision that God is not glorified whenever one of his churches closes its doors

- Forming a team to commit time and energy researching available options and understanding our situation in more detail

- Committing our future entirely to God's leadership and guidance and seeking his direction for our future, faithfully keeping it before him in our prayers

- Providing regular and frequent communication before the church, so they were fully aware of all activities that were taking place by the CCR team

- Allowing God to reveal his will by opening or closing doors, and then obediently following his direction

While the final results of this decision are still to come in our future, we are very confident that God has a plan for this church that will far exceed any of our enthusiastic expectations. We are committed to align ourselves with his will and allow him the opportunity to do what he does best—save lost souls by grace through faith in his glorious Son!

- Calvary Church Nampa

DISCUSSION QUESTIONS

1. The Lord's strength is perfect in our weakness. Which of the verses shared at the beginning of this chapter brings you the most hope for your church's situation in this time? Why?

2. In this chapter, we considered five next steps for you and your church to take as you seek to discern God's leading. Spend some time strategizing for how you are going to follow through on, and carry out, each of these five steps:

   - **Step #1:** *Seek God's leading through prayer and Scripture.*
   - **Step #2:** *Honestly evaluate your church's current condition.*
   - **Step #3:** *Pursue counsel and wisdom from outside of your church.*
   - **Step #4:** *Bring a recommendation to your congregation.*
   - **Step #5:** *Trust God and move forward in humility and faith.*

3. Take the time right now to pray about how the Lord wants to work in your church's situation. Pray for wisdom and clarity as you may be talking with a variety of leaders and pastors who want to be of help to your church. Whom should you contact first?

Appendix

HOW CAN WE FIND THE RIGHT SENDING CHURCH?

Earlier in this book, I introduced the idea of replanting through a sending congregation. While this option is not always possible, I am convinced it gives the potential replant its best chance for long-haul health and renewed multiplication. However, deciding you want to replant through a sending congregation isn't enough. You need the right sending congregation to partner with. But how can you tell if a potential sending church is the right fit?

I've included this appendix to offer you some practical tools in discerning if a potential sending congregation is the right one for your church. Hopefully, you already have a congregation in mind and have even reached out to explore what it might look like to partner together. If not, the same groups I mentioned in Chapter 7 (denominational & network leaders; local seminaries & Bible schools; local pastors & churches) may be of great help.

Once a congregation expresses interest, I encourage you in combination with other leaders in your church to begin answering the following questions honestly. If you are not able to answer them immediately, that's okay! But, don't skip past this stage. Take some time to compile what information you can, so that through prayer, discernment, and discussion you can determine how best to move forward.

When Evaluating a Sending Church:
9 Questions to Discuss

1. **Readiness.** First, is YOUR congregation ready to be replanted, or are you still a few years out?

2. **Theology.** Where is there alignment in theology? Where is there not?

3. **Secondary Matters.** What secondary values, convictions, and traditions are shared between your congregations? Which ones are not shared? Which of these secondary matters are you willing to change in order to move forward?

4. **Finances.** What financial roadblocks might stand in the way of your partnership? Are there major building repairs which need to take place? Have you been transparent about your financial circumstances?

5. **Denomination/Networks.** Are there any denominational or network conflicts that could hinder your partnership? What expectations come with the resources they might offer.

6. **Leadership.** Do you feel you can trust their leaders? How have they demonstrated their trustworthiness? Do you have any initial concerns with their motives or readiness?

7. **Strategy.** What is their plan for replanting your congregation? Is it well thought-out? Tested? Has this church ever done something like this before?

8. **Community.** How well do they know the unique neighborhood you are in? How will they help you to better reach the individuals and families around you? Does it have a vision for multiplication beyond your church?

9. Legacy. Have they taken time to learn the history of your church? Are they aware of both the bright points and the dark spots? What pieces of your past do you need to be honest about? Which pieces of your legacy would you like to see carry on?

Before you can answer these questions, however, you must be aware of what your "negotiables" and your "non-negotiables" are as a congregation. Surprisingly, these can be difficult to put your finger on, but you must be clear on them in order to move forward. The following tool has been developed to help your leaders clarify these convictions and determine whether to continue conversations with a potential sending church. It is simply called, **"The Discernment Grid."**

Negotiables						Non-Negotiables									THE DISCERNMENT GRID
Existing Programs	Existing Staff	Worship Style	Finances	Building	Lord's Supper (frequency)	Baptism	Church Leadership	Day to Day Operations	Growth Strategy	Denominational Alignment	Philosophy of Ministry	Philosophy of Mission	Theology	Church Polity & Government	
															Red (unwillingness)
															Yellow (openness)
															Green (supportiveness)

HOW THE DISCERNMENT GRID WORKS

Negotiable vs. Non-Negotiable

As you look along the left side of the Discernment Grid, you will see the two primary categories we are working with, those things that are negotiable when considering potentially partnering with this congregation and those things that are non-negotiable. If something falls into the negotiable category, it means this is something that while important to consider and be aware of, this is not an issue that will make or break moving forward in discussion with this church. It falls into the realm of, "Let's agree to disagree agreeably." On the other hand, if something falls into the non-negotiable category, it means this is an issue that must be agreed upon and aligned with or else moving forward to explore replanting together is an impossibility.

You may choose to rearrange this list of non-negotiables vs. negotiables to better reflect the values and convictions of your church. Perhaps you will add some new ones and take out some of those I have proposed. That is fine. This is simply a tool to help you and your church in the discernment process.

While our heart is to see your church be replanted by a sending church, we also realize that when we don't align in these specific areas with the dying church, the trajectories of the churches are very different, and it's better to say "No" from the beginning. Perhaps there is another sending church that will be a better fit for you. After many conversations with many churches of all types, here are some of the most common convictions that are mentioned.

Non-Negotiables

- **Church Polity & Government:** The basic leadership and authority structure of the congregation as laid out in the by-laws.

- **Theology:** The core doctrinal beliefs of the congregation.

- **Philosophy of Mission:** The congregation's understanding and practice of mission, specifically as it relates to engaging culture and the lost with the gospel.

- **Philosophy of Ministry:** The congregation's understanding and application of biblical teaching to the practice of practical ministry.

- **Denominational Alignment:** The congregation's affiliation with a particular denomination.

- **Growth Strategy:** The vision and strategy of the congregation in regard to future growth and multiplication.

- **Day-to-Day Operations:** The practical, day to day, leadership and decision making of the congregation.

- **Church Leadership:** The role of the lead pastor-elder and other pastor-elders within the congregation.

- **Baptism:** The congregation's theology and practice of baptism.

Negotiables

- **Lord's Supper (Frequency):** The congregation's practice of the Lord's Supper, specifically its frequency.

- **Building:** The condition of the physical building and all surrounding property belonging to the congregation.

- **Finances:** The financial situation of the church including its savings, debt, monthly expenses, and monthly income.

- **Worship Style:** The style of worship, specifically music, experienced each week in the worship service.

- **Existing Staff:** The individuals who are currently on paid staff at the church and their roles.

- **Existing Programs:** The existing, active programs of the congregation for children, youth, and adults.

Red vs. Yellow vs. Green

Once you have decided on your core list of both non-negotiables and negotiables, you will move on to the rating scale. You will notice along the top of the grid, moving from left to right, three rating colors: Red, Yellow, and Green. Simply put, you will rate the potential sending church regarding their alignment with each of your non-negotiables and negotiables (it functions like a stoplight). The ratings are:

- **Red:** The potential sending church is unwilling to align with your church on this non-negotiable or negotiable issue.

- **Yellow:** The potential sending church is open to alignment with your church on this non-negotiable or negotiable issue.

- **Green:** The potential sending church is supportive in aligning with your church on this non-negotiable or negotiable issue.

So how exactly do you rate this church's readiness to replant in light of the data you have gathered and put into the Discernment Grid? The following rating scale can help you in this.

The Rating Scale

Red church:

There are one or more red ratings in the non-negotiable areas or three or more red ratings in the negotiables category.

> **What this means...** If the potential sending church receives a red rating, it is unwise to move forward in pursuit of replanting with this congregation. There is simply not enough alignment on major things between the two churches to make it work.

Yellow church:

There are one or more yellow ratings in the non-negotiable areas or three or more yellow ratings in the negotiables category.

> **What this means...** If the sending church receives a yellow rating, your church may choose to move forward and continue

conversation with this congregation but you must do so slowly and with caution. There is alignment on most things, but there are still areas of misalignment that need to be further assessed and discussed. You may talk as a church about what it could look like to partner with this church in other ways than replanting. It might be helpful to have a more distant relationship with them to walk alongside them & share resources, rather than a replanting situation where you are fully partnered together.

Green church:

A Green Church means all non-negotiable & negotiable areas are rated in the green. There might be one or two areas from the negotiable list that are yellow and you just have to lead the congregation in those areas, helping them to understand what the goal is.

> **What this means...** There is huge potential for your church to partner with this sending church. You are aligned in all major areas and next steps forward together should be taken.

THE BOTTOM LINE

Spend some time filling in and discussing the Discernment Grid as leaders of the legacy congregtion. Again, the hope is that this will assist you in clearly identifying the potential of pursuing partnership with this potential sending church.

The bottom line in all of this is that you want to take seriously the step of evaluating and assessing a church's readiness for replanting your congregation. You want to know what you are getting into, for good and bad. You want to have a good feel for the culture of the church before you and your congregation decide to move forward to replant and revitalize, and asking good questions can help you honestly evaluate the partnership potential

BIBLIOGRAPHY

Altrogge, Stephen. "8 Prayers You Should Pray for Your Pastor." *The Blazing Center,* March 21, 2017. Accessed August 15, 2017, http://theblazingcenter.com/2017/03/pray-for-your-pastor.html

"Associational Replant Guide," *The North American Mission Board,* April 7, 2017. Accessed August 15, 2017. https://www.namb.net/resources/replant-associational-guide.

Clifton, Mark. "Dying Churches Matter to God....and to NAMB." *The North American Mission Board,* January 26, 2015. Accessed September 1, 2016. https://www.namb.net/send-network-blog/dying-churches-matter-to-god-and-to-namb.

Clifton, Mark. *Reclaiming Glory: Creating a Gospel Legacy throughout North America.* Nashville, TN: B&H Publishing Group, 2016.

Henard, Bill. *Can These Bones Live?: A Practical Guide to Church Revitalization.* Nashville, TN: B&H Publishing Group, 2015.

McKinley, Mike. "The Pros and Cons of Planting and Revitalization," *9 Marks,* October 27, 2011. Accessed June 13, 2016. https://9marks.org/article/journalpros-and-cons-planting-and-revitalizing/.

Moher, Al. "A Guide to Church Revitalization," *Southern Baptist Theological Seminary.* Accessed January 7, 2017. http://www.sbts.edu/press/a-guide-to-church-revitalization/#download.

Schmucker, Matt. "Why Revitalize?" *9 Marks,* October, 27, 2011. Accessed August 5, 2016. https://9marks.org/article/journalwhy-revitalize/.

Spurgeon, Charles. "Made Perfect in Weakness," *Truth for Life,* November 4, 1881. Accessed November 4, 2016. https://www.truthforlife.org/resources/daily-devotionals/11/4/1881/.

Warren, Rick. "The Five Stages of Renewal in the Local Church." *Pastors.com*, March 19, 2015. Accessed August 15, 2017. http://pastors.com/the-five-stages-of-renewal-in-the-local-church/.

Wilhite, Shawn. "7 Ways to Care for your Pastor." *The Gospel Coalition*, February 11, 2016. Assessed May 17, 2017. https://www.thegospelcoalition.org/article/7-ways-to-care-for-your-pastor.

NOTES

Chapter1: What is Church Replanting?

[1] Al Moher. "A Guide to Church Revitalization," SBTS.edu, accessed January 7, 2017, http://www.sbts.edu/press/a-guide-to-church-revitalization/#download.

[2] See the NAMB "Associational Replant Guide" for more on the differences between revitalization and replanting. "Associational Replant Guide," The North American Mission Board, April 7, 2017, accessed August 15, 2017, https://www.namb.net/resources/replant-associational-guide.

Chapter 2: Why Should We Consider Replanting Our Church?

[1] Matt Schmucker, "Why Revitalize?", *9 Marks*, October, 27, 2011, accessed August 5, 2016. https://9marks.org/article/journalwhy-revitalize/.

[2] Ibid.

[3] Mark Clifton, "Dying Churches Matter to God....and to NAMB", *The North American Mission Board*, January 26, 2015, accessed September 1, 2016. https://www.namb.net/send-network-blog/dying-churches-matter-to-god-and-to-namb.

Chapter 3: What Does God Say about Churches Like Ours?

[1] Charles Spurgeon, "Made Perfect In Weakness," *Truth for Life*, November 4, 1881, accessed November 4, 2016, https://www.truthforlife.org/resources/daily-devotionals/11/4/1881/.

[2] Ibid.

[3] Ibid.

[4] Bill Henard, *Can These Bones Live?: A Practical Guide to Church Revitalization* (Nashville, TN: B&H Publishing Group, 2015), 2.

[5] Ibid.

[6] Mark Clifton, "Dying Churches Matter to God."

⁷ See Rick Warren's article, "The Five Stages of Renewal in the Local Church." Rick Warren, "The Five Stages of Renewal in the Local Church," *Pastors.com*, March 19, 2015, accessed August 15, 2017, http://pastors.com/the-five-stages-of-renewal-in-the-local-church/.

⁸ Ibid.

Chapter 5: Is Our Church Ready to Be Replanted?

¹ Mark Clifton, *Reclaiming Glory: Creating a Gospel Legacy throughout North America* (Nashville: B&H, 2016), 23.

² Mike McKinley, "The Pros and Cons of Planting and Revitalization," *9Marks*, October 27, 2011, accessed June 13, 2016, https://9marks.org/article/journalpros-and-cons-planting-and-revitalizing/.

³ Clifton, *Reclaiming Glory*, 25.

⁴ McKinley, "The Pros and Cons."

Chapter 6: What Role Can I Play?

¹ Shawn Wilhite, "7 Ways to Care for your Pastor," *The Gospel Coalition*, February 11, 2016, assessed May 17, 2017, https://www.thegospelcoalition.org/article/7-ways-to-care-for-your-pastor.

² Adapted from Stephen Altrogge, "8 Prayers You Should Pray for Your Pastor," *The Blazing Center*, March 21, 2017, accessed August 15, 2017, http://theblazingcenter.com/2017/03/pray-for-your-pastor.html.

³ Ben Haley writing on the importance of rest and renewal for pastors through intentional Sabbath keeping.

Chapter 7: What's Next?

¹ Mark Clifton, *Reclaiming Glory*, 31.

the Replant Series

This series features short, action-oriented resources aimed at equipping the North American church for a movement of church replanting, introduced by Pastor Mark Hallock's book *Replant Roadmap*.

Thousands of churches are closing their doors in United States every year in some of its fastest-growing, most under-reached neighborhoods. Yet there is much hope for these churches, particularly through the biblically-rooted, gospel-saturated work of replanting.

Designed for both group and individual study, these books will help you understand what the Bible has to say about how God builds and strengthens his church and offer you some practical steps toward revitalization in your own.

For more information, visit **acomapress.org** and **nonignorable.org**

ACOMA PRESS

Acoma Press exists to make Jesus non-ignorable by equipping and encouraging churches through gospel-centered resources.

Toward this end, each purchase of an Acoma Press resource serves to catalyze disciple-making and to equip leaders in God's Church. In fact, a portion of your purchase goes directly to funding planting and replanting efforts in North America and beyond. To see more of our current resources, visit us at *acomapress.org*.

Thank you.

Made in the USA
Columbia, SC
12 February 2021

32818721R00085